I0081805

Experience
The Joy of Spirituality

Secrets of the Doorway Home
The secrets of life are like seeds
Seeds of Light you plant within
You nurture them
They blossom to illumine you

through

Meditations

for the

Journey into Light

Book Nine
Finding your Purpose

Carl Mohan

Meditations for the Journey into Light
Copyright © 2017 Carl Mohan

All rights reserved. No part of this publication may be reproduced or transmitted in any form or by any means, graphic, mechanical, electronic, including photocopying, recording, taping, information storage or retrieval systems, or otherwise, without prior written approval from the author.

Cover design and interior formatting by Tugboat Design

ISBN: 978-0-9782970-0-8

Vision Dreamer
Guelph Ontario Canada
vision.dreamer@yahoo.ca

Dedication

This book is dedicated to my mother and father. They are examples of their beliefs, which were manifested in their lives. Anyone who can dedicate such commitment to their life has exceeded that state of simply being a parent and member of a society. When you find aspects of someone's life you can choose to emulate, then you have found someone who walks as a teacher in the truest sense.

Walk along the path of Truth
With a heart filled with Love
And journey into Light

Table of Contents

Brief Contents

Preface

I have come to realize that my existence has been shaped simply by the choices that I have made. All I am is a result of the choices that I have made on my journey through time. In my search for Truth I have been faced with many challenges. I have learned that the challenges I confront each day offer choices. Each choice represents a different pathway. In my journey onward, I have followed many different pathways, some filled with joy; some, sorrow and hardship. I have gained knowledge and wisdom along the way. I have learned that wisdom cannot be gained from books, or teachers or Spirit guides. It comes from experience. It comes from living. I have learned that it takes strength and courage to choose. When you choose, you gain experience. It is through such experience that you gain wisdom.

I have learned how to use wisdom to navigate my physical life and that the spiritual path is navigated not by wisdom but by a compass that points in a different direction. It is the direction of spiritual joy. I have learned that all of life is one. All of existence is connected. Knowledge, Truth and wisdom belong to no one. It belongs to all. As consciousness expands, it embraces all knowledge, all Truth and all wisdom. It embraces a realm of totality where all such things belong to everyone. This is the nature of oneness and the foundation of joy.

I owe a great deal of gratitude to many. During the early part of my journey, I encountered the works of Edgar Cayce *(March 18, 1887 - January 3, 1945)*, a psychic from Hopkinsville, Kentucky,

USA, which laid a foundation upon which I have based much of my life. It has directed me on a pathway that opened many new doors. I was blessed to have encountered many teachers along the way who appeared at a time when most needed, scattering seeds which took root as I faced the challenges which navigated shaped my journey in life. Particularly noteworthy was a powerful aboriginal teacher and shaman. Together with her friends, she offered much to give me hope in the essence of life. I owe much gratitude to the many who offered Truth, which integrated into the very cells of my being. Every teacher, every experience and every challenge added to the flavour of my being, of whom I am today.

I have discovered that the mental framework, which is developed during the formative years in this realm, is the result of the mental, emotional and spiritual framework of parents, family and friends. Our Spirit uses this framework as a foundation for manifesting in the physical, for the opportunities and challenges desired by Spirit to expand life here in this realm and beyond.

I have learned that life is about growing and expanding to embrace all that I am. It is the direction of the compass of spiritual joy. I have chosen to embark on this journey into Light. I have chosen to follow the path of spiritual joy. It is a path founded upon Love and Truth, which leads to totality. I invite you to join me on this amazing journey into Light.

These pages that follow are the words of my heart, which is the voice of my Spirit and the essence of my being. It is my prayer that these words carry a spark of Light which will touch your heart and illumine you as I feel them within mine. It is my prayer that all of humanity will realize the power that is held within as beings of Light shining from beyond, manifesting here in this realm. By listening to the voice of your Spirit, you manifest this Light of life, which is your very essence, here in this, your physical existence.

Acknowledgments

I am grateful to the many who read the manuscript and offered encouragement. I am grateful to the ones who read it and offered editorial changes. I am grateful to the ones who offered the promise of success.

It is so easy to doubt yourself. Transcending doubt is one of the great challenges of life, offering lessons of courage, acceptance, Love and faith in the self. To the many who walked with me on the road to victory, you are dearly remembered and acknowledged with a smile in my heart.

The smile in the hearts of those who are blessed by this book will be the reward of all who contributed.

Introduction

Why do you depend on history for answers when life is about the now, this moment, this breath and what you choose to do with the energy you inhale with each breath? Archaeologists, historians, biblical scholars all offer views of what life has been and how life should be. Governments, churches and industry all practise forms of slavery by offering frameworks whereby control can be established to reap material rewards for this physical existence. As you explore life, the Truth can bring much pain. However, Truth is the fabric of existence and the foundation of your being. Intrinsic to your growth into Light is the acceptance of Truth. It is one of the first steps on the journey upward and onward into Light.

There is no single or golden path. Your journey here has been unique with a series of unique experiences. Likewise, the return journey will also be unique. You are a being of Light. You are the total of all your experiences from the time of your inception into Light. That part of your being that is Spirit seeks to return to the Light.

You have journeyed to a place in your reality where that part of your being which is mind is not aware of your Spirit. The desires of Spirit are spoken within the silence of your conscious mind. It is your own Spirit that infuses the innate desire to embrace the state of spiritual joy, infused by your own Spirit, which seeds feeling of emptiness, loneliness and incompleteness. Awareness of these feelings serve as a beacon on your journey in life.

What is spiritual joy? It is a state of being in which you feel complete. It is a state of life filled with meaning, in which emptiness or loneliness ends. The desire to find "something more" ends. It is a state in which Spirit unites with the flesh in singleness of purpose. You embark on a journey guided only by your Spirit. It is a state filled with Light.

A life of joy is like a diamond with numerous facets gleaming like a brilliant rainbow of sparkling Light. How do you get there from here? The answer is simple. You choose it then you manifest it.

As you read this book each chapter will address one colour in the rainbow of Light, a facet of the diamond that you are, and if you choose to follow the guidance it inspires within, you will embark on this very personal journey of awakening.

Journey onward with patience as you take time to read, pray and meditate. You will find fulfillment and your Spirit will fly free, sparkling with eternal joy.

Organization of This Book

Through time and with patience, as you become aware of the secrets of your life's journey, past experiences may appear to be random, but like the journey of the sun across the sky each day, there is order in all of existence. What may not be immediately obvious can be essential and intrinsic to your being, such as the Light of the sun as an essential source of life to this realm. As you take a closer look at your own life, you will see that there is order and progression.

The chapters of this book may not appear sequential, but collectively they form a unit, which parallels the progression of your very own life as outlined in the "Prayer to our Father." (This prayer is discussed later and forms the basis of this book.) Each chapter and each section may be viewed as independent units, units of Truth, which will touch different parts of your being. Your life is unique, with unique needs and challenges; thus, what you may find of importance will change as you progress along this journey you call life.

Do not be disturbed by repetition. In this book, you will find much. To understand the reason, consider the purpose of recurrent dreams or the parable shared by the Nazarene Master in the Book of Luke, chapter 11, verses 5-13.

The importance cannot be emphasized enough. To reap the benefits of this book, read it slowly. Like good food, chew upon it with patience, tasting with your entire being the morsels of Truth and Love held within each word, phrase and chapter. Your very life depends on the nourishment, not only for the body and mind, but also for the Spirit's journey onward. Each chapter and word has been chosen with care, so it may touch your Spirit, opening the door to enlightenment. You are Light, born of Light. This book is designed to nurture and open doors so you may feel the dance of Light within the very foundation of your being.

The chapters of this book parallel the seven expressions of your totality. Seven symbolizes perfection. When all seven are in balance, Spirit and flesh become unified. It is the state you call enlightenment when the Light of the Spirit shines through the flesh.

There are seven chapters. Each expression of your totality is addressed by a chapter, highlighting a different area of your being, where Spirit touches the flesh, manifesting physical life. By addressing the spiritual and physical health of these areas, a doorway opens, allowing the Light of the Spirit to penetrate and shine upon the flesh, uniting Spirit and flesh as one.

Spirit is perfect. Remember that you are already perfect in every way. Know that you are loved by the very fabric of existence. You are fully and completely accepted. Choose to open your eyes, realize this Love and live it.

Each chapter offers a tool — meditation — which will help you open this door. As you practise meditation, be prepared to walk through a door, which will take you away from the comfort zone of the flesh as defined by the mind. You will embark on a journey which leads you to extraordinary places where you will experience such freedom your Spirit will soar like the eagles on high.

In addition to *meditations*, each chapter offers *prayers*, *reflections*, *illuminations* and *lessons*, all of which are intrinsically similar but address different aspects of your being. All appeal to the nature of your higher self in the expression of oneness with life here in this realm.

A *prayer* can be viewed as an appeal to your own spirit, the angels and all of creation or what some define as God, for some form of assistance or guidance. *Prayer* sets in motion forces which are not seen by physical eyes. *Prayer* is an appeal that employs words either vocally, or spoken within the mind.

Reflection and contemplation are much the same. It is an appeal to your higher self for answers to a specific question. It is a process by which the mind is presented with a question or situation. The answers then flow into your consciousness and are received by the mind. It is a source of deeper understanding. This process does not involve words.

Illumination is a state of being. It is achieved when meditation is successful. Some view it as enlightenment. It is a state in which you are embraced by the Light of your Spirit and all of creation. With eyes of Spirit, you can see the Light, which illumines your being. You can feel the words of Love and Truth which surround you.

The *lessons* offered in this book are words of wisdom, which you may use for your life's journey. Each challenge you face in life offers lessons. Lessons become the wisdom, which navigate your pathway. Seek the Truth that the lessons offer for your journey. Read them, pray about them, reflect, meditate, and they will illumine you.

Meditation offers answers. The early stages can involve prayer and reflection, then the process of seeking transformation, followed by illumination. Meditation is a doorway. It reveals a path on which you fulfill your purpose for being here in this realm. Successful meditation goes beyond illumination to embrace your natural state of Love and Truth, illumined by the Light of your Spirit. This pathway is the life you live. It is the journey onward and upward into Light.

The ancient masters practised meditation to free their Spirits from the bonds of the flesh. The one known as the Master, who emerged from Nazareth, taught his followers how to use meditation and explore the connection between flesh and Spirit. The format of this book is based on a meditation taught by this ancient Master. Take and eat of this body of Truth and it will set you free.

If you choose, look upon this book as a symbol of your life, each chapter being a phase or component of your being; each section representing a challenge; each word representing your own thoughts. When you open it, indeed it is a mirror upon which you gaze, and it offers guidance to a place that you seek, the Light that you are.

Be blessed in body, mind and Spirit as you undertake this journey of challenges. Like the Nazarene Master who challenged himself to be all that he is, you are also on a journey of challenges. Challenge yourself to be all that you are. On the busy highway of life that you are currently travelling, challenge yourself to stop and re-examine the map, and chart a new course that will take you onward and upward into Light.

The Stairway to Heaven

It has taken several years to compile this book. The word "compile" is used because this book is a collection of many different works penned over seven long years. It even includes *Buds of Light (Appendix B),* which shine from the beyond. From the writings, I can see how I have changed and grown. The variety of experiences and challenges brought Truth to my doorstep. It is this vein of this Truth which flows through the book.

The stairway to heaven is paved with such Truths. Perhaps this book will help you find Truth on your journey. Each Truth you embrace is a step forward. Each step takes you closer to the Light. It takes one small step at a time to climb the ladder of life.

If you find difficulty in understanding this book, fear not. The journey to the end of the rainbow, searching for that elusive pot of gold, requires faith. It is this faith which manifests the strength and courage to pursue what the mind tells you is only an illusion. The mind is simply a tool and does not have the ability to embrace the fullness of the Spirit. This book shows how you can open the doorway to the Spirit. It requires faith to transcend the limits and boundaries created by the mind. It takes faith to climb the stairway to a heavenly consciousness where you shine with all your brilliance.

Born of Light, the consciousness you now embrace is a result of the multitude of trials and tribulations which you experienced on the sinuous journey of existence. The return journey to the Light will also be as unique as the one that brought you here. This book will help you open the doors so your Spirit can guide you along a path paved with the Truth revealed to you.

Finding Your Purpose

You ask of your purpose. The answer is simple, but are you prepared to receive it? Be forewarned that it is one of great challenge, hope and despair, but you have the power to undertake this journey.

It is a journey of experience, one that started with your birth into Light. You have travelled here to experience the touch of three dimensions. You have experienced joy and you have experienced the valley of shadows. You now seek your way back to the Light to once again embrace the fullness of your Spirit.

The Source of Truth

Realize that the source of all Truth is within. Once you see this, you will no longer need this book or any other book. This book will assist in many ways. It will help you see this Truth. It will show you how to open the doorway of your heart, which leads onward and upward into Light, to a place you once called your home.

Is the reward worth the effort? Ask yourself this question. Is there anything thing else more worthwhile in life? Allow your Spirit to answer.

Foundation

The Prayer to our Father

As you seek Truth, it is the presence of your Spirit within which will embrace you and offer answers, guiding, protecting and inspiring you, every step of the way.

In 1947 a significant archaeological find was a multitude of scrolls, hidden in caves for more than two millennia, beside the silent waters of the Dead Sea. The scrolls were biblical in nature and covered many books of the Bible. It took scholars several years to decipher the decaying documents, but what was unearthed offered a new perspective on religion and spirituality.

One of the scrolls contained a short prayer called: "The Prayer to Our Father." It was written in the ancient language of Aramaic. Today, there are many different translations. In Western society, one of the most common versions is know as "The Lord's Prayer" and is found in the King James Version of the Bible.

Aramaic was the main language in that part of the world at the time. Like English, Aramaic was a complicated language in which one word or phrase could have several different meanings, all influenced by variables such as culture and religion. Historically, Aramaic documents were first translated into Greek, then Latin and finally into English. Without knowledge of the traditions at the time when the scrolls were written or translated, the Truth could easily remain hidden.

Over the years, changes surrounding social, moral, religious and political structures have resulted in multiple revisions of the Bible. The church of today and biblical scholars offer various interpretations. Although the study of the various translations reveals how different they are, within the depth of each, the same basic Truth emerges.

The Bible is filled with a multitude of symbols. Used as a means of communication, symbols can transcend time, culture and religion. Symbols in the Bible, such as those found in "The Prayer to Our Father," reveal Truths which relate to life today.

The world has changed in many ways, morally, technologically and physically. Traditions of today are vastly different from ancient times. However, there is much that transcends time. The essence of your Spirit remains unchanged. The energy of your emotions remains unchanged. The power of Love, Light, colour, Truth and joy that is the foundation of your being transcends time.

The Bible reveals Truths regarding the physical body and its relationship with the spiritual realm. It reveals ways the mind can be used to unite the two as one. The mind cannot fully comprehend the Spirit realm but reflects like a mirror what it experiences through the physical senses.

Why do some remember past lives? It is because Spirit sees and knows all. The awareness of Spirit transcends the limits of the body, mind, time and indeed, this physical life. Spirit is conscious of all lifetimes. If you are ready and willing to open your eyes and see as Spirit, you also can embrace the consciousness of lives beyond this physical experience. You will embrace a consciousness which holds a broad perspective of reality and a source of Truth which transcends time.

Why do some see the future? With the eyes of Spirit, there is an awareness of what lies beyond the veil of this physical life. There is an awareness of past and present, which offers a probability of what the future will hold. Astrology can also impact the direction of humankind, but people have free will to choose, regardless of any such influence. The doorway to the future opens when the eyes of your Spirit are open.

What is the relationship between this Truth and your personal life? What is the relationship between Truth and wisdom? Some describe wisdom as "insight." Biblical scholars speak of the "Wisdom of Solomon." The wise man will choose, based on both spiritual Truths and personal experience. In the Bible, the wisdom hidden within the words incorporates spiritual Truth of our vast experience through time. *It is your power to choose which gives you complete command of your life.* It is this wisdom which will navigate your journey onward and upward into Light.

Spirit communicates wisdom to the mind using the language of symbols. Symbols can be quite personal, for example, a rose to someone could mean Love and beauty as seen in the colour and softness of the petals, while to another it may mean pain and suffering as symbolized by the sharp thorns. Biblical scholars face the added dimension of time and culture. Even today, if you consider translating French to English, it may appear to be a straightforward task. For example, there are many differences between French from Quebec and French from France that have evolved due to vastly different customs and traditions. Similarly, an English-speaking Englishman or Englishwoman may be unable to communicate with an English-speaking Jamaican because of the different dialects and intonations, although the origin of the language is the same.

This is also true of much of the Bible. Without the luxury of a spoken language, Spirit is attempting the complex task of addressing dynamic social structures with timeless messages, so the people of yesterday, today and tomorrow can gain an understanding of life.

What happens to the Truth when ego comes into play? If you examine the original text of the Bible, which was not written in English, you will find the translations of today have been re-worked, re-written, massaged, revised and changed many times. In this century alone, it has been revised at least seventy times. Controversy over its correctness still persists today. For example, when homosexuality sought a place in mainstream society, the ripples caused debate regarding the correctness of words such as "man" and "woman." Also, the infusion of the concept of "terrorism" within society seeded concern regarding sections that could be interpreted as "hate." Can you imagine the impact of the political, social and religious framework of the writers of the Bible? No wonder there is so much difficulty in understanding its purpose and finding the Truth hidden within its pages. If you are seeking ways to use it for your personal agenda, what will you find? If you are earnestly looking for the Truth shrouded by time and tradition, what will you find?

Within the Bible, there are four gospels. Each tells the same story but in a slightly different way. Each offers a different perspective of the same Truth, giving the reader the opportunity to gain a more thorough understanding of life. The gospels provide four different facets of life, which can be explored further in the sixth chapter of the Book of Revelation.

"The Prayer to Our Father" appears both in the Book of Matthew and the Book of Luke, but they are different. In today's society, the translation most are familiar with comes from Matthew. In this book, the version in Luke will be explored. Although each translation is different, what is important to note is that there are seven significant lines or sections in each translation.

The following translation of "The Prayer to Our Father" was taken from Luke, chapter 11, verses 1-4 of the King James Version of the Bible. Note that seven significant words are underlined which will be addressed later.

> *Our Father which art in <u>heaven</u>,*
> *Hallowed be thy <u>name</u>.*
> *Thy kingdom come.*
> *Thy <u>will</u> be done, as in heaven, so in earth.*
> *Give us day by day our daily <u>bread</u>.*
> *And forgive us our <u>debts</u>; for we also forgive every one that is indebted to us.*

And lead us not into <u>temptation</u>;
But deliver us from <u>evil</u>.

What is the true purpose and meaning of this "prayer"? Why was it given? What remains hidden behind tradition and religious dogma? What endures beyond the view of the physical mind? What secrets have the words and symbols held for more than a millennium?

It is widely accepted that a Nazarene called Yeshua, known today as Jesus, gave "The Prayer to Our Father" in ancient times. He was a learned man, a Master and scholar. The Muslim world know of him as "al-MaseeHu `Eesa," which means "Jesus the Messiah." It is in Hebrew that he was known as Yeshua. In Greek, he was known as Iesous. In Latin, the word used was Iesus. In India, he was called Essa. The name "Jesus" appears only in the modern English translations of the Bible. (In this book, he is referred to as the "Nazarene Master.")

Within the complexity of life today, many feel enslaved by a creedal legacy and have embarked on a search for freedom. What has happened to the teachings of the Nazarene Master and how do they relate to religion and your life? When you look at churches, you find empty pews because many have abandoned their connection with mainstream religion. Many feel enslaved by a framework of creeds in which there is no substance and in which traditions and rituals serve not the Spirit of Love and Truth but the ways of the flesh, eclipsing dreams of hope and joy. Many carry scars of this legacy and find it difficult to journey onward.

However, there are answers. It takes time, sometimes a lifetime of seeking to find answers that satisfy the deep inner yearning of your Spirit. It can take lifetime to find Truth, which will restore your faith in life. Hidden within the words of the "Prayer to Our Father" is such Truth. Even beyond this, hidden within your own heart, you will find eternal Truths. If for a moment you can choose to listen to your heart, the instrument of Love and Truth, what will it reveal? If you can ignore all the mind offers in the name of religion, science, philosophy or reason, and set aside the framework of traditions and rituals which you carry from the past, and focus only on your heart, what will you hear? You will hear the voice of your very own Spirit, which speaks within the silence of your heart and offers a new perspective, one defined not by tradition, but based on eternal Truths.

There were many great teachers in the past, such as Mohammed, Buddha, Mahatma Gandhi and Moses. If you travel back in time even further, you will find ones such as Plato, Thoth and Hermes of Atlantis. Many religions have been founded upon the philosophies of such teachers and masters.

Ask yourself these questions: Why do you have religions? Who started religions and for what purpose? Do religions offer hope and joy? Do religions actually offer the Truth, which frees the Spirit that you may journey onward and upward into Light? Allow the voice of your own Spirit, which speaks within your heart, to answer these questions.

Your Spirit will reveal to you that eternal Truth exists everywhere in the vast garden of life. It is where dreams of hope and joy are born. If you choose to open the door, they will become your reality. It is a place where you will find seeds of Light starting to bud, and as you nurture them, they will blossom into Truth and Love that will illumine you, from within.

Such are the secrets of life. Many such secrets have been offered by the teachers of the past. The pattern or example known in society today lies within the one who came before, walked the streets of Nazareth, challenging himself to be all that he is and achieved the level of "Master" because of spiritual and physical accomplishments. His whole life demonstrated that the greatest source of Truth is what your Spirit offers from within.

His example demonstrates that progress through the journey of life expands the consciousness to embrace realms of Truth beyond this physical domain. His life exemplifies a power so great that it is seen today as unnatural to human beings. The spiritual Truths which he demonstrates bestow a joy that surpasses understanding. Thus, he became an example for humanity, which transcends time.

His example attracted seekers from far and wide. It is his example that seeded many religions of today.

How can his life be put into the perspective of today's framework of creeds? When your consciousness expands to embrace Truth from the realms beyond the physical, it is labelled *psychic*. The Webster dictionary describe *psychic* as "spiritual in origin." Some consider it a spiritual gift. Those who have this ability to "channel" spiritual truths, which can be verified, become famous and attract a multitude of seekers. A Sunday school teacher from Kentucky, USA called Edgar Cayce became one of the world's most famous modern day psychics.

Although the accomplishments of the Nazarene Master cannot be compared with any modern-day psychic, in much the same way, many followed after him as he walked along the dusty streets of Nazareth. His ability to offer Truth was unsurpassed. His demonstration of wisdom, compassion and Love for everyone was incomparable. It is no wonder that his fame spread far and wide. Seekers flocked from everywhere to find him.

There were many other teachers at the time who were also wise, healed and offered spiritual Truths. The followers of one called John were being taught how to meditate, heal and do readings. His students could successfully demonstrate their newfound ability to channel spiritual Truth.

The young Nazarene Master was a sprightly, robust and energetic fellow with long matted hair, a beard, strange clothes and brisk walk. Many today have seen him through visions and dreams. His students wanted to learn, much like the students of the other teacher who was gaining fame, the one called John. Matthew and Luke, according to the translations of the ancient documents, recorded that the students asked to be taught how to "pray." Mark and John, writers of the other gospels, did not include the "prayer" in their records. They were perhaps out fishing for the tribe on that particular day, so they missed the lesson.

It was the custom of teachers to ask for questions. The students who became interested in John's teaching also wanted to learn how to heal and channel spiritual Truths, so they seized the opportunity and asked their beloved friend YESHUA to teach them how to "pray." This is where the story began, for they received far more than what was asked.

No different from any kindergarten teacher now who would tell stories, in addition to sharing "The Prayer to Our Father," the young Nazarene Master shared lessons to aid its understanding. According to the King James Version, the Book of Luke, chapter 11, verses 5-13, these were some of his words.

5. *And he said unto them, Which of you shall have a friend, and shall go unto him at midnight, and say unto him, Friend, lend me three loaves;*

6. *For a friend of mine in his journey is come to me, and I have nothing to set before him?*

7. *And he from within shall answer and say, Trouble me not: the door is now shut, and my children are with me in bed; I cannot rise and give thee.*

8. *I say unto you, Though he will not rise and give him, because he is his friend, yet because of his importunity [troublesomely urgent or persistent in requesting] he will rise and give him as many as he needeth.*

9. *And I say unto you, ask, and it shall be given you; seek, and ye shall find; knock, and it shall be opened unto you.*

10. *For everyone that asketh receiveth; and he that seeketh findeth; and to him that knocketh it shall be opened.*

Here, the Nazarene Master discusses the importance of being persistent in order to be successful in your quest. He also talks of the inner Light, which is symbolized by the word "bread."

11. *If a son [daughter] shall ask bread of any of you that is a <u>father</u>, will he give him a stone? Or if he ask a fish, will he for a fish [bread] give him a serpent [temptation]?*

12. *Or if he shall ask an egg, will he offer him a scorpion?*

13. *If yes; then, being evil, know how to give good gifts unto your children: how much more shall God the Father give the <u>Spirit</u> to them that ask him?*

The Nazarene Master also reveals that it is your Spirit which knows your deep desires, and you will receive beyond what is asked, but first, you must honour your Spirit and choose to ask.

To reap the fruits of hope and joy, the Bible teaches that you need to seek with persistence. You need to take action, for it is your choice, your free will. The converse is also true, for if you do not take action, you will remain lost within the creedal legacy, which you embrace.

The young Master indeed saw beyond the words of his students and offered Truths, which address not only their questions but also the desires of their Spirits. "The Prayer to Our Father" is not simply a "prayer" in the traditional sense. According to the Edgar Cayce material, it is a very deep and powerful meditation whereby the symbols within the seven lines of the "prayer," or rather meditation, address the seven spiritual centres of your being. Each centre is a doorway, or an interface, between the physical and spiritual. Each centre is a link between body and Spirit. From a scientific perspective, each spiritual centre corresponds with one or more of the endocrine glands. In Hindu philosophy, the centres are called chakras, a Sanskrit word meaning rotating wheel. The energy within continually moves, expands, rotates and grows, which is life, your life.

The endocrine glands each hold a specific function which governs the development of the physical body. The energies, which govern each of the glands, maintain the physical, mental and spiritual state of your being. By altering the nature of these energies, you can change the totality of your being. It is your innate power. Herein lies the purpose of meditation and "The Prayer to Our Father."

The endocrine system, or chakra system, can be viewed as the Biblical "burning bush" or the Cabalistic "tree of life." Each gland is connected one with the other, and they all work together in harmony. The flow of energy is up and down as directed by the highest source, or pituitary. In meditation, the tree comes alive with the inextinguishable fire of life. It can happen all at once, or it can be a gradual enlightening experience. Realize that you are already a body of Light and what you seek in meditation is the brilliance of this burning fire of life.

In this meditation, you receive guidance from your very own Spirit. You are led along a path of challenges. If you choose to open the door, the challenges become opportunities, providing growth and transformation. Growth that is both physical and spiritual. As you embrace your spiritual purpose, the endocrine system manifests physical transformation.

To explore each of the seven centres fully would require many volumes, and perhaps many lifetimes. There are seven chapters in this book and each addresses one line of the "prayer." Collectively, they show the relationship between the "prayer," the endocrine system and how to open the doorway. This leads to the oneness of mind, body and Spirit, thereby achieving your purpose here in this realm. They show you how to embrace your spiritual power and fly free. With a true commitment to yourself, you have the power within this lifetime to fly free, onward and upward into Light.

The first line of the prayer, "Our Father which art in heaven," focuses on the seventh or crown chakra. It corresponds with the pituitary gland, located at the base of the brain. The pituitary generates hormones, which can stimulate other glands of the endocrine system. The symbol to keep in mind is "heaven." Heaven is the blissful consciousness of your true essence. It is in this area of your being where all components of your life become balanced and function as one. As you meditate, embrace your own Spirit and the totality of your being as you expand your consciousness to unite with all as one.

The second line of the prayer, "Hallowed be thy name" focuses on the sixth chakra. It corresponds with the pineal gland, located deep within the brain. In Hindu philosophy, it is described as the "third eye." It is the area within your being where your vision expands beyond the perception of the physical realm to reveal what is not seen by eyes of flesh. The symbol to keep in mind is "name." Your true "name" represents the energy of your highest aspirations. It is the desire of your Spirit to unite this energy with your physicality. Viewed from another perspective, as the "third eye" opens, you become aware of a hidden part of your being, your essence. You gain the realization that you have travelled long and far and have lived many different and unique lives, each with a unique name. One "name" existed from the beginning, at the time of your birth into Light, which represents your true essence. It is the sacred place of blissful consciousness you seek to embrace in this step of the meditation.

The third line, "Thy Kingdom come, thy will be done, as in heaven, so in earth" focuses on the fifth chakra. It corresponds with the thyroid gland, located at the base of the neck. The symbol to keep in mind is "will," the power to choose. The thyroid gland is controlled by the pituitary, or seventh chakra. At this state of your meditation, the energy from the sixth chakra is pouring downwards onto the fifth, energizing and expanding your power to choose. Choice is your free "will." What will you choose to manifest? Yes, you do have a choice, for the forces which press upon your being are many, and all seek expression. Will you choose Spirit or flesh? To shine with the burning fires of life that flow from above (your heavenly consciousness), choose the way of the Spirit and manifest your highest aspirations in the realms below (your physicality). Life guided by the Light from above is everlasting.

The fourth line, "Give us this day our daily bread" focuses on the first chakra in the body of Light. It corresponds with the reproductive glands, testes in the male and ovaries in the female. These glands produce sex hormones. The symbol to keep in mind is "bread." Why bread? Directed by the pituitary, these hormones seed the building blocks of physical life. With the guidance of Spirit, you become the creator of your reality, past, present and future.

The building blocks of life require sustenance or "bread" that is both physical and spiritual. In the multi-dimensional process of creation, it is in this area of your being where flesh and Spirit unite to create an expression of life in three dimensions. Purpose, attitudes and aspirations unite with the flesh, guided by the will, to determine the nature of life you manifest. In this stage of the meditation, it is the Light flowing from above, all the way down to the first chakra, which is the source and determining pattern of life you manifest.

The fifth line, "And forgive us our debts; for we also forgive every one that is indebted to us," focuses on the third chakra. It corresponds with the adrenal glands. The symbol to keep in mind is "debts." Debts are patterns which you have embraced but no longer serve the purpose of your Spirit. They have become an innate part of your being. At this stage of your meditation, the third chakra becomes active, awakening cellular memory which reveals these patterns, some seeded in this lifetime and beyond. Hindu philosophy describes it as karma. As old patterns emerge, you are presented with the opportunity to once again choose. You face the challenge of the acceptance of self and others. You face the challenges of your own fears. The Light flowing from above offers you strength and courage. It is the opportunity to choose differently, thereby unlocking karmic ties. Each new pattern takes you one step closer to the doorway of freedom from the cycle of re-birth.

The sixth line, "And lead us not into temptation," focuses on the second chakra. It corresponds with the leydig cells, which remain inactive until puberty. The symbol to keep in mind is "tempta-tion." It is the area where physical desires emerge and ego seeks expression. What will you choose to create? What will you choose to glorify: Spirit or flesh? Will you choose to manifest your spiri-tual desires by embracing your highest aspirations, uniting them with your physical energies? Channelling your physical energies into spiritual creativity requires your courage and power to choose Spirit over flesh. In this stage of the meditation, Light from above passes through the fifth chakra, filling your being with the courage and power to choose. You can feel the energy flow up and down as you embrace the power of your Spirit to overcome temptations of the flesh, and shine with the Light of creation in all your actions.

The seventh and last line of the prayer, "But deliver us from evil," focuses on the fourth chakra. It corresponds with the thymus, located in the heart area. The symbol to keep in mind is "deliverer." This is the area of spiritual Love. It forms a bridge between the upper and lower chakras. As the energy from above pours onto the fourth chakra, it becomes infused with the transforming power of Love. This energy then flows down upon the lower three chakras. Once again, you have a choice. Will you choose to embrace all the activities of the lower three chakras with the Love that is offered from above? Love becomes the "deliverer" from evil or temptations of the flesh. If you so choose, spiritual Love is the power which will restore balance. At this stage of your meditation, you shine like a "tree of light," burning with the brilliance of your Spirit, balancing the totality of your being.

In summary, the upper three chakras relate to the phrase, "as it is in heaven," from the "The Prayer to Our Father" and the lower three chakras relate to the phrase "thy will be done on earth." As the upper three chakras are activated, inner guidance offers the awareness of your true nature which you can choose to manifest in the physical realm, through the lower three chakras. This philosophy and Truth date back to ancient Atlantis. "As above, so below," was written on the Emerald Tablet of Hermes.

It is the Nazarene Master who showed how the tempering and transforming power of spiritual Love bridges the upper and lower chakras. He showed that the pattern is in the burning tree of Light, which you also hold within. "The Prayer to Our Father" is a representation of the flow of energy in the manifestation of life. The flow starts with Spirit at the crown, or seventh chakra, snakes its way down to the base, or first chakra, and then moves all the way up to the heart, or fourth chakra. Realize that your Spirit is a spark from the eternal Light of God. When the Light touches your crown you are at one, not only with your Spirit, but also with God and all of creation. You are at one with all of life. You need only to open your eyes, the eyes of your Spirit to see this.

The human body is truly an amazing instrument of the Spirit. According to medical science, the endocrine glands form a unit responsible for the production of hormones. Hormones are chemicals which affect every aspect of body function, from reproduction to health and longevity. The term hormone means "To set into motion." When the endocrine glands or chakras become active, hormones are secreted into the blood system. Minute amounts of hormones can have a significant effect on bodily changes. Love, anger, pride etc., activate the endocrine glands, initiating the production of hormones which impact both negatively and positively upon your state of being. If you tell a lie, it impacts the endocrine glands and generates hormones. What will it set into motion? Do you know how many years it will take from your life? When you Love, or become a peacemaker, can you imagine the extent of the healing power you are manifesting within your own being?

In ancient times, many lived hundreds and even thousands of years. You can now see how this is possible. When Spirit is at the helm, the flesh becomes limitless. Spirit is limitless. However, with the awareness of what lies beyond, why would you choose to experience this realm beyond what is absolutely necessary?

It is your life. Is Spirit at the helm? The true purpose of this meditation is to activate the endocrine system, producing hormones which manifest in the physicality, attitudes and choices of Spirit, bringing transformation on the journey onward and upward in Light.

If you choose to use this meditation or any form of meditation, it is important to first gain an understanding of your true purpose. In meditation, you become free from the protections of the mind. When this happens, it is your purpose that will guide and protect you from undesirable forces and energies that may seek to use you for their expression. You have been shown a door. If you walk in, it is by choice. If you choose, let your will be guided by your own

Spirit, the source of eternal Truth.

Meditation is truly a powerful and an amazing tool, which has been hidden from your eyes by clouds of tradition. The teachings of the Nazarene Master symbolize the conquering of the mind by Spirit. The mind is no longer subject to the wants and desires of the physical realm. Spirit instead guides the mind. The spiritualized mind becomes limitless, free from the restrictions and boundaries of the physical realm.

Meditation is only part of the process of spiritualizing the mind. It requires your choice and your action. Activating the endocrine glands in meditation allows you to see beyond the limitations of the mind. When your purpose is in accordance with spiritual laws, you become aware of the steps which are required. Since each Spirit is unique and experiences unique lives with a host of unique situations, your attachment to this realm is also unique. It will take courage and strength to undo these attachments, thereby freeing the mind. The limitless mind transcends the physical and Spirit flies free.

How does this relate to life today? You face challenges in your life every day and each moment. You are constantly looking for answers. You are searching even if you realize it or not. You have searched everywhere. You have an innate knowledge that there is a greater Truth, and you seek to embrace fully all which is Truth. You are looking for ways to guide your life to a higher purpose.

What happens when you sit in meditation? Do you wonder what life is all about? Do you look at the moon, stars and trees, and expand your consciousness as far as you can to embrace the sun, the universe and all that is beyond? Do you wonder if universes revolve around a central sun? There is so much beauty and wonder abound and you are part of it all. Your Spirit embraces all of it. Spirit embraces all of existence. Spirit embraces the consciousness of all life.

When you listen to your Spirit, to the voices you hear within, to the impressions you receive, to the emotions you feel, do questions arise regarding Spirit and flesh and their relationship? How

15

are they integrated? Where do you find such answers? Know that all you feel from Spirit is real and realize that the flesh passes back to the dust from where it came.

The world around you may confuse you and seek to draw you away from what is real. You may look around and see governments that seek to control. You see the pain and suffering of little children. Do you see the gradual loss of freedom? Do you see people's inhumanity to each other? Within all this, however, it is a wonderful consolation to stop for a moment and contemplate the purity of the universe and Spirit. It is wonderful to recall that you are a unique Spirit, responsible for your own life, and you have the potential to be all that you choose. It is a consolation to remember the power you hold within which you command through your chakras, and no one can take this away from you.

The connection between your Spirit and God is eternal. No matter how difficult the walk in flesh may become, you can always meditate. You can unite as one with the Light from above, pouring down upon you, and in the sanctuary of the seventh chakra, there to find the freedom of Love and Truth, nourished by the embrace of God's golden Light. Amen.

Illumination

Seeds of Light

You are Light.
Seeds
Ready to blossom.

Choose now
This path.

Nourished by Truth and Love
Growing
Changing.

Blossoms
See them grow.

Blossoms of Light.
Blossoms of joy.

Blossoming into life
All that you are.

Prayer

Divine Creator, I give thanks for Love and Light. I give thanks for Truth. I give thanks for the "bread" which nourishes and enlightens the Spirit.

I give thanks for the presence of Spirit in my life. I give thanks for the guidance of Spirit, which offers transformation and enlightenment.

I pray that the angels walk with me, to guide, council and protect me. I pray for the blessing of the Light, which burns from within to enlighten me with the brilliance of Love and Truth.

I give thanks for the "Prayer to Our Father" and seek understanding that I may receive the Truth that it offers, to guide me on my journey, onward and upward into Light.

Enlighten me as I meditate upon the Truth that the words offer.

The Prayer to Our Father
Our Father which art in heaven,
Hallowed be thy name.
Thy kingdom come.
Thy will be done on earth, as in heaven.
Give us day by day our daily bread.
And forgive us our debts; as we forgive our debtors.
And lead us not into temptation; but deliver us from evil.
For thine is the kingdom, the power and the glory, forever and ever.
Amen.

Chapter One

As It Is in Heaven

Introduction

Light is everywhere. Open your eyes and you will see the sparkling and glimmering colours of Love that spiral around you. Feel the joy of being in the presence of and touched by this Light.

The energy from within emerges and interacts with the chakras, travelling up and down and throughout your body, dancing to the rhythm of your thoughts, actions and choices, reflecting colours that are a visible energy field around your body. This is known as the aura. The energy from the totality of existence which surrounds you awaits your invitation to unite in oneness. As you choose to experience Spirit and flesh as one, the energy flows down though your crown, intertwining with your life force and illuminating your entire being like a tree of Light which shines with a rainbow of colour from within. As you meditate and expand your consciousness to manifest the desire of Spirit, you are seen as Light. All that exists is seen as Light cradled by a consciousness, which is Love and Truth. Like a child with outstretched arms reaching for his/her parent, oneness with this all-embracing Light is the innate desire of the Spirit within.

With free will, you can move in any direction you choose. You have chosen to journey to a place of oneness with the all-embracing

Light. It is choice which brought you to this realm of the flesh, and you have the power to return once again to the place where flesh and Spirit unite as one in the dance of life. You have the power to transcend this realm, fly free and return to the place your Spirit calls home.

Once you understand that oneness with Spirit is your sole purpose in this physical realm, your attitude towards life changes. Your physicality becomes a tool used by Spirit to manifest Love and Truth. Your physicality becomes a tool of healing by dissolving old patterns and re-building your life with a foundation of Love and Truth. The value your mind has placed on physical objectives becomes diminished and in oneness, responds only to commands from the Spirit.

Once you have journeyed to this place of Light where Spirit and flesh unite as one, your energy will grow as a brilliant white Light filled with hues of violet and gold. You will feel the power of the Light radiate from within every energy centre. You will feel the all-embracing Light surround you and merge with every cell of your being. You will feel Love flowing from the depths of your being, reaching out to touch someone and everyone. You will feel the healing power of Love reaching out to embrace your life and all life. You will feel the joy that is eternal.

Sparkling with White, Violet and Gold

Many around you have agendas and seek to draw you into the drama of their lives, pulling you away from the path you have chosen to walk. They choose to exercise their power to control. It feels like they are kicking at the proverbial horse upon which you are riding, expecting you to fall into their hold. You have fallen before, many times, but to your credit, you have promptly climbed back on, determined to continue onward, on the journey you have chosen, undefeated.

Such interference makes the journey difficult, but you have

come to realize that these are the challenges that tempt the flesh and temper the Spirit. You have persevered and have chosen your path and are ready and willing to continue on the journey, despite the hindrances encountered along the way. When you make such a choice, you feel your power expand in readiness to face the unknown. You feel prepared to manifest the essence of your being, the source of Love and Truth. Truth is the foundation and fabric of your being. Love is acceptance without condition or judgment. Love is never controlling. Love and Truth become the crowning glory of your being. They become the essence of all your intentions, the source of your power and the foundation of all that you create.

Kings and queens wear crowns of jewels, each with a unique colour and shape. The jewels are symbols of power. Larger and numerous jewels symbolize greater power.

Realize that you also wear a crown, one shaped by your own power. It is the true crown. Choices, aspirations and achievements all determine the type of crown you possess. When viewed from the perspective of Spirit, we understand that we are all beings of Light and all shine with brilliant colours that emanate from the energy, which emerges from within. This energy is your power and such power is your crowning glory.

As you grow and transcend the flesh, you learn that there is energy in all things. As you touch what seems like the most insignificant grain of sand, you feel its energy. This can even be verified by scientific methods, with the use of an electron microscope whereby the structure of the sand is seen in its elemental form as neutrons, electrons and protons, which is all energy. The framework of science requires machines for justification. To walk as Spirit, such justification is not needed. Spirit impresses it upon your consciousness.

Your life is governed by a consciousness in which Truth is the substance and Love, the creative force. The energy, which manifests as a grain of sand, is also governed by a consciousness. Embracing all that exists is a consciousness governed by Love and Truth. The ancients describe this as the one God or Creator of life.

Meditation is a tool to unite your unique consciousness with the all-embracing energy or consciousness of the totality of life. Each cell within your physical and spiritual body will dance with joy as you unite once more [as it was in the beginning] with this energy. It enters through the crown and permeates your entire being. You will feel the transforming power within as your consciousness expands to embrace the foundation of Love and Truth. You will be bathed in a warmth and joy that cannot be described with words which will travel to the depth of your being. A healing balm will embrace you. You will shine. Your aura will be filled with purple, white and gold. Such is the journey onward and upward to the all-embracing Light.

Seventh Chakra Meditation

In this meditation, place your focus on the area of the seventh chakra. The symbol to keep in mind is "heaven." The seventh chakra corresponds with the pituitary, a gland that sits at the base of the brain. When this area is activated, a channel to the Creator of life opens and the area around your head becomes encircled with Light.

As you meditate with your eyes closed, you can stop the buzz of the mind and the world around you when you place your focus on this area of your being. You can <u>feel</u> the silence of existence. You can <u>feel</u> the unity and oneness with the energy of the Creator of life. You become aware of the guidance and inspiration that is flowing into your consciousness.

Recall once again the words of the Nazarene Master: "Our Father, which art in <u>heaven</u>." As you meditate upon these words, realize that "heaven" emerges out of a state of being or a consciousness, one not limited by the physical realm or mind. It is the consciousness, which is the Light you embraced at your birth into reality. It is that part of your being which is the Creator of your life. The innate purpose of your journey is the emergence of the Light, which is your blueprint. You are a Light seeking to manifest your spiritual consciousness not only in your meditations, but also as a function of your mind, as you project into the physical realm clothed in flesh.

Meditation brings growth and change. As you choose while in meditation, call upon your mind to do likewise, manifesting your choice in the physical world. Embrace the Light of your Spirit and allow it to command the mind. Your goal as a student of spirituality is to make choices that bring growth and transformation, both in meditation and in every moment. Always maintain the energy and eagerness of a student. As you grow, let each breath fuel your power to choose the way of Spirit. As you shine during meditation, learn how to hold this aura in each moment. Hold strong your power to choose Love and Truth in each moment and with each breath.

As you choose to manifest on Earth, "as it is in heaven," this area becomes more and more luminous, emitting such a brilliant glow of the purest and whitest Light which encircles your head and flows down to embrace your entire being and the world around you.

Embraced by the Light

It is time for you to start a new venture, a journey into Light. The meditation which follows will prepare you for what is to come. In Truth, the journey has already begun. You have been seeking Light your entire life. Your whole existence has been one of seeking. From the time of your inception into reality, you felt the embrace of the golden Light of creation, out of which you emerged. From that experience you became aware of the feeling of its embrace.

You have journeyed afar, away from the warmth of the Light, and now you seek to return and reconnect with what is now a distant and almost lost memory. This memory beckons from deep within, calling you to again embrace the peace and joy that you once knew, something which the flesh alone cannot provide.

The inner gnawing is ever present, each day, every moment, fuelling a fire of seeking. At times, you feel that the search is in vain, for time after time the results offered only false happiness, which disappeared like smoke, bringing disappointment after disappointment, but the inner gnawing and the search continue.

Perhaps you have not yet realized that you may be looking in the wrong place. Perhaps you have not yet realized that what you seek cannot be found here in this realm. Perhaps you have not realized that the gnawing from within is an inward-seeking search for something that you once knew in the beginning.

Where do you find such happiness that will not fade as the evening sun? What do you have to do to find contentment, fulfil-ment, peace, satisfaction and true joy? How do you find the elusive eternal bliss?

You must realize that everyone in this realm is on a different and unique journey. You have journeyed long and far with experiences that have taken you meandering through time and space. Now, the inner gnawing is calling for you to return, to journey back. The return journey will be as unique as the one that brought you to where you are now, one defined by the unique nature of your Spirit. There is no simple, secret or golden pathway. The path that leads to the Light, which is ever before you, is always the answer. How do you find the doorway and embark on this sacred journey?

Perhaps the answer will become simple and clear once you have truly made the commitment to listen to the voice from within. You will become aware of the path to eternal bliss when you choose to ready your vessel, your body, mind and Spirit.

It is true that such thoughts bring much despair to the heart of one who is so deeply wearied from a long and arduous journey. You question yourself.

"Why does it not make any sense?"

"Am I less than the beings around me?"

"Am I totally lost without hope of return?"

"Is there an answer for this wearied Spirit?"

Yes. The answer is a resounding yes. You seek to walk the path, which leads out of the valley of shadows to a place where you will feel the warmth of the eternal Light, warmth that is truly blissful. Each person, no matter who you are, holds that spark within, a spark that is filled with hope, Love and Truth, a spark that is the very source of your life, which will grow bright and become one with the eternal Light.

In this meditation, choose to become one with the eternal Light which flows from the totality of existence to unite with your life force. Listen to the guiding energies, which accept you without condition, expectation or judgment and offer you a cup that is overflowing with Love and Truth. Take and drink and become quenched, nourished in body, mind and Spirit.

Meditation of the Spirit
And so dearly beloved one, it is time to relax.
Go into a place that is your sanctuary and find your sacred place
    of relaxation.
Relax your body.
Relax your mind.
Relax and listen.
Listen for voice of your heart.
Stop the buzz of the world around you and listen.
Focus on the area of your heart and listen.
Feel the serenity that silence offers.
Accept this blessing.

There are noises around you that seek to distract you. These are the sounds of cars, distant voices, footsteps, sirens, the whisper of the wind, birds chirping, falling leaves, the gentle trickle of a stream, flowers swaying gently in the breeze, the hum of nothingness, but realize that these are all far away and no longer have power over you. Your mind will not heed their call. Go deep into the silence of your heart, the sanctuary of your being, and know that these sounds are all far away, from a different place and a distant realm.

Take a deep and gentle breath, and as you exhale, slow down.

Take another deep and gentle breath, and as you exhale, from the quiet of the mind, listen to the blissful silence of your heart.

Take a deep and gentle breath, and as you slowly and gently exhale, close your eyes and listen. Listen for the rhythmic beating of your heart.

Take a deep and gentle breath, and as you slowly and gently exhale, listen for the sound of the earth beneath you. Listen for her rhythmic heartbeat.

Take a deep and gentle breath,and as you slowly and gently exhale, listen to the rhythmic music of the spheres.

As you attune to the music, make comfortable, controlled, continuous, connected and gentle breaths. Keep your focus on the area of your heart. Feel the beat of your heart. Feel the pump of blood carrying warmth, peace and life through your entire body.

Breathe gently and comfortably as you feel the life force within.

Feel the beat of your heart. As you listen to the music of your heart, allow yourself to relax even more.

Allow all doubts and fears of the mind to go with the wind. Know that you are being guided and there is nothing to fear. You may choose just to let go, knowing that you are safe and protected. Just let go. Let go of all that you choose. Let your thoughts go. Let your worries go. Free yourself from anything and everything that seeks to distract the mind. Let it be taken away by the gentle breeze to a distant shore. See them fly far away like dandelion seed tendrils. No fears. No concerns. No worries. You are in this moment, totally relaxed and free as the wind. You are in command of your being. You are here now. You are at peace. You are one with the fullness of life. Prepare to go deep within.

Prayer

Divine Creator of life, I ask that you bless this time of meditation. I ask that you embrace me with your Love, guidance and Light of protection. Guide me to find all that I seek. Guide me to that place where the eternal Light burns deep within. Amen.

Take a gentle breath, and as you exhale, relax and go to that place of total peace.

As you focus on the beat of your heart, place your focus on the rhythm of your breathing. Feel the energy of life as it flows into your body, nourishing every cell. Feel the energy of life flowing within as you breathe.

Feel the rhythm of your breath. Feel the air as it fills your lungs, nourishing your body with life-giving energy. Feel the air leave your lungs as you exhale. Feel the purity of energy fill your lungs as you inhale. Feel the energy diffuse into your body. As you exhale, feel your lungs empty completely. Notice the sensations and feelings as you inhale. Notice the sensation as you exhale.

Breathe in the Light

You are in a place of deep relaxation. You are embraced by the power to leave the material world behind. As you exhale, use your will to send your fears far away. With faith, command them to leave. Allow the eternal Light to take their place. Ask for the healing Light to come in and embrace you.

Now you are at peace. You have found that place of inner serenity. Feel the embrace and oneness of the Light.

As you breathe, inhale the Light. Allow it to enter your body. Allow it to fill your lungs. Allow it to flow into your veins. Allow it to touch every cell and every organ. Allow it to invigorate and enliven the totality of your being. Allow it to infuse healing energy within. Allow it to bring into your being that aura of peace.

Take a moment to pray silently for guidance.

Prayer

Divine Creator of life, I ask for a blessing as I seek to be in the presence of your Light. I pray for guidance and direction as I search for peace and joy and happiness. Allow me to fill my lungs with your Light that I may be blessed with the healing balm of your eternal Love.

I ask that you watch over and protect me at this time. I ask for the angels to come forth and stand with me, forming a circle of protection around me. I ask that the pathway to eternal Light be open before me. I ask that I may find the guidance to walk forth in your Light. Amen.

The State of Calm

Feel the embrace of the eternal Light. Embrace that state of peace and joy the Light offers. Feel it infuse within to create a state of bliss.

As you breathe, feel the Light.

Feel the warmth of the Light.

Feel the beauty that is the Light.

Feel the infusing power of all the colours of Light.

Feel the transformation, as you become Light.

You are a being of Light shining from within.

You are glowing.

Every cell of your being is glowing with the purest and whitest Light, emitting a rainbow of colour.

Feel the state of calm that the Light emits within your being.

With each breath, go into a deeper state of calm.

Go deep, deep, deep into the deepest state of calm.

As you feel the silence, as you feel the calm, which extends beyond the boundaries of the flesh, go into an even deeper state of calm. Command your mind to BE STILL.

Love

Go beyond the state of calm, even deeper, to the state of pure Love. Allow your Spirit to infuse your mind with Love. You are Love. Every breath you take is energized by Love. You are energized by Love. All that you are is energy, which is Love.

You can feel everything, yet nothing. Know this feeling. Know this place. Embrace it all, for it is the state of oneness. This you can take back with you when you return to your physicality. Remember this feeling, remember this place and embrace it, so you may return empowered by the totality of your being.

Return

It is time to return to the physical realm. Take a gentle breath and realize that you are a Light. Remember that you can always seek this path, the one which leads to the Light within, which unites as one with all that is eternal. Accept the blessings of all that you have received. Know that all you have received is the Truth. Know that Truth is but a door which leads to the Light of your Spirit.

Realize that Love and Light is life. Realize it is who you are. Realize it is your birthright.

Be at peace always. Know that you are loved without condition or expectation by a heavenly host. Choose to accept the Love and Light that flows from the fountain of life, embracing you, always.

It is time to return now to the physical realm, to your physical existence, to the awareness of your physicality, to the consciousness of your physical body. In gentleness, as you breathe, journey back. When you are ready, take a gentle breath as you open your eyes, conscious of your physical existence, refreshed, empowered by Love and embraced by the blessings of the Light that you have received.

Prayer
I give thanks for the embrace of Light so I may journey onward and upward with the power to manifest Love and Truth in all my thoughts and actions. I pray that the angels walk with me on my journey, behind me to protect me, beside me to council me and before me to show me the way. I pray for the strength and courage to walk the path of Truth, embrace the power of Love, nourished by Love, empowered by Love, to manifest all that I AM, now and always. Amen.

Reflection

Seek Ye First

Seek ye first the kingdom of God
And its righteousness
And all these things shall be added unto you.

But I say unto you
Where is this kingdom?

Know the Truth that it is within
Seen with eyes of the Spirit
Felt by the hands of the Spirit
Known by the consciousness of the Spirit.

Awaken to this Truth.
Live life according to this Truth.

For you seek God.
You seek the kingdom.
You seek heaven.

For it is not here
It is within.

Prayer

Prayer of Light

I give thanks for the Light that embraces all.

I give thanks for the Love which embraces the universe and all of existence and which flows through my veins, bringing Light to my life.

I give thanks that I may embrace this Light and feel the Love that shines everywhere.

I give thanks for Truth.

I ask that I may embrace the Light, which shines as Truth, and feel the Truth that is the foundation of existence.

I give thanks for peace.

I ask that my eyes may be opened so I see and feel the Light that shines in peace. I ask that all of humanity may embrace the Light of peace.

I ask that I may embrace the Light, which is Love and Truth and peace, the Light that unites all of humanity as one.

I ask that I may embrace in oneness the eternal Light of life so I may journey onward and upward onto eternal joy, now and always.

I ask that my life may be an example that all of humanity finds the joy which is within.

Amen.

Illumination

The Dance of Light

You are a musical instrument.
You dance to a rhythm.
The beat of your feelings.
Your desires and emotions.
Radiating a rainbow of colour and Light.

Shining with your brilliance
As you play and dance
And orchestrate
The music of your life.
Amen.

Each day brings the sparkle of new Light, only to realize that the Light which dances in the glory of the morning is eternal. So it is with you. You are an eternal Light. What you shine through the flesh is your choice.

How do you feel in the moment and what are you prepared to do to sparkle like the morning sun? Realize that you are a Light, and like the sun, you shine eternally. Joy is your birthright. Fear not. Open your heart and dance to the rhythm of your life. It is simply a choice that you make. Let each breath energize your life. Let each breath manifest the voice of your Spirit and sing the song of Love and Truth as you dance.

Let your life be a dance of Light for you are Light. You were born to dance. You entered this realm to dance. Thus, sing and dance with all your might for it is your life, and what you do is your choice. Choose wisely.

Meditation

Victory is Mine

Live the "I AM."
Choose this.
It is mine to command.

I am Love.
I am Truth.
I am one with the Light of life.

In this moment
In every moment
Live the "I AM."
Choose this.
It is mine to command.
Amen.

The passage of time is to be savoured, as your life is flavoured by the essence of your being, giving each breath value and purpose. You are as you choose; thus, let your choice be guided by the essence of who you are, navigating your life into the Light. Victory is being who you are. Realize that the "I AM" is the essence of who you are, Love and Truth. To realize the I AM is bliss. Victory is bliss. Choose to let the passage of time be the nourishment for your being which creates bliss. Amen.

Each challenge you face offers the opportunity for a victory. Spirit over flesh, to one day conquer the flesh and achieve the state of bliss. Amen.

Prayer

Prayer for the Traveller

I give thanks that I can be here at this moment to share the Love that you have bestowed upon humankind, and that I can make it part of my being as I travel the pathway of Truth on my journey each day. Walk with me, talk with me and guide me on my way. Be the protecting Light, which surrounds me in all that I do and say, now and forever more as I journey onward and upward. Amen.

Remember to pray each day. You can choose to be prayerful in each moment. Your life is defined by your choice and choice is a function of your Spirit. Choice is simply a birthright given by the Creator of life. As you choose, it is your Spirit that chooses. Fear not. Realize that your mind will seek control. Within there is the knowingness of Spirit. Spirit is Truth and Love. Spirit offers the path to eternal bliss. Thus choose.

Engineer your life as you choose to manifest your aspirations by speaking these words as an appeal to yourself. In the humility of speaking, words take wings and fly to the ears of your totality and to all who unite with you and share your aspirations.

Many pray without even realizing it. Know that your thoughts which form the foundation of your spiritual aspirations are defined as prayer. Thoughts which hold an attitude of expectedness are powerful prayers.

Reflection

Message for the Journey

What do you feel?
It is simple as that.
Then walk the journey of feelings.

Feelings are your Truth.
Each one a seed.
Ready to blossom.

The garden of your life is before you.
Fertile is the soil.
Love is the sustenance.

Plant the seeds
To blossom into joy
With all the colours of the rainbow.

For it is your life.
The seeds of Truth you grow
And blossom into Light.

Lesson 01

All That You Are

The challenges that you face make you who you are. The greater the challenge, the stronger you become. The greater the challenge, the wiser you become. The greater the challenge, the more experienced you become. The greater the challenge, the more courageous you become. You grow in power. You shine in your brilliance.

The Light you shine brings joy and beauty to life. It brings joy and beauty to all who are touched by the warmth of your Light.

Prayer

Prayer of Love

Reach out and touch me
With a Light that consumes me
That I may be filled
That I may feel the union with Light
And become one with all.
Amen.

Lesson 02

Love and Truth

Listen to the words of your Sprit
Spoken in the silence of your heart.

"Truth does not control.
Truth embraces all.
Truth brings growth and transformation.

You are a Guardian.
You are a Student.
You are a Messenger.
You are a Witness.

Share not the Truth of this path.
Nor seek pride-fully of this."

For it is your secret
Your power
And your Truth.

Your task
And tomorrow the unyielding example.
Amen.

Illumination

I am and Will Be

I am who I am
I am Love and will always be Love
I am Truth and will always be Truth

Truth is the foundation of reality
It is the substance of the heart
It is the building blocks of the Spirit
It is the essence of my being

Love nurtures
Love creates
Love unites
Love builds

I will be all that I am in Love and Truth
To embrace life
To embrace all that partakes of life
To unite as one with life

Lesson 03

It Is Truth

Union with the Light is the opportunity to grow, as seeds that fall to the ground from God's trees, ready to take root.

Reflection

The Spirit of Truth

Find that place where Spirit unites with the consciousness. It is a place of guidance. It is a place of Love. It is the place from where life emerges. It is here you grow and change and become all that you are. This is the place you seek in meditation; the place you seek in life.

Illumination

God's Embrace

To embrace your Spirit is to embrace life. To know Spirit is to embrace the feelings of Love and Truth. Your feelings flow through the heart centre, the doorway to the higher consciousness.

The mind is the consciousness of your physicality and the physical realm. Its view of reality is derived from the senses. It is the voice of reason.

Existence extends beyond the realm of reason. Life extends far beyond the reaches of the mind. The consciousness that embraces all extends from a place the mind cannot perceive. It is the consciousness which is embraced by the heart centre.

Meditate upon the silence of your heart, the centre of your being, and you will walk through the doorway, which leads to the higher consciousness. There the Creator of life will embrace you.

Amen.

Reflection

Finding Your Purpose

It is being who you are.
It is being all that you are.
Here and now
In this very moment.

It is a journey to that place
Where you are all that you are
Here and now
In this very moment.

Illumination

The Path of Oneness

In the beginning, I was one.
Then there were two.
I seek once again to become one.
My Spirit seeks you.

That which you are shines.
That which I am shines.

That which you are is joy.
That which I am is joy.

Your Spirit feels my Light.
My Spirit feels your Light.
Together we are one in Light.
Shining brighter.

Love is the unity of Light.
In the unity of Light there is new life.
In the unity of Light there is joy.

Reflection

The Secret Doctrine of the Christ

How do you live a life worthy as shown in the doctrine of the Christ? It is not a secret or hidden doctrine, but one available to anyone willing to receive it.

What must you do if you are truly willing to receive this doctrine? How must you change your life?

Each life can be viewed as a flower. Choose to open your eyes to see it.

The story of the young girl who angrily left her home because of an uncaring mother, realized when it was too late, through her own experiences of motherhood, that she had judged her mother unfairly. Her mother's actions were actually based on a deep Love.

If you are willing to look beyond anger and pain, you will see the Spirit of Love within each life. The flame may be weak and in need of nourishment, but it is there. If eyes cannot see, then they have no purpose. It is the Spirit within that gives the eyes purpose to look beyond the flesh.

Find the Truth within your own heart and there you will find the Light. It is a Light which shines within all. Find the Light within your own heart, manifest it and in so doing teach your children likewise.

Reflection

The New Tomorrow

Now is the time to speak the Truth regarding who you are and all that is to come. In meditation, as you leave this world behind and look to the Truth that flows from that one source, it brings forth all that is to be known. A voice from deep within emerges to bring Light where there is fear, that Truth may embrace all and raise the vibration of the world, that the vision of a new reality may become manifest.

Realize that you are creating your futures. What you do and say and think and imagine creates your tomorrow, and collective tomorrows are the future of the world. What you do today, what you do now in this moment sets waves into motion that will become the future. This has been the reality from the beginning of time. You are experiencing history as it repeats itself, and will do so over and over again.

Will you not open your eyes and learn from the past? Instead of repeating the cycle, end old patterns that no longer serve Spirit. In meditation, you have been shown the Light. Realize you are the Light. Open your eyes and your heart and embrace the Light.

You know the Truth. You already know the result if you choose to once again walk the ways of the past. It is time to transcend old patterns and instead choose to embrace Truth, which is offered by the Light, which shines from within your own Spirit. You have the power within to shine this Light, balancing, neutralizing and clearing the way for a new tomorrow. Oceans may rise and fall. Lands may erode, but the Light from your heart will always shine, and it is with your choice and your will that this Light may become manifest. It is simple. Use your best wisdom, embraced by the Light, to choose the path you walk and manifest a future you desire.

What do you see in the future? Is it great oceans surrounded by white sand and towering infernos of Light pouring down upon the meek and lowly and bringing harmony to the lives of all? Everyone garbed in white, free from the chains of the flesh, amidst the glory and glitter of a new reality? You see children playing in the streets without fear. Gold scattered everywhere is of no consequence: children use them as toys. The trees, skies and great domes light up. Everyone gleaming like a jewelled crown, a new beginning, growing, expanding, encompassing all, the entire Earth, healing and transforming. All things become new. The voices of the angels ring out from the heavens in musical harmony. Bliss is a word that is not known, for it is the reality, the wave, which flows through all and nothing else is known. The waters of life course like rivers, sparkling, pure and clear, amongst lush gardens and trees that deposit petals upon the gentle waters, where birds sing sympatico with the angelic host.

A mighty one walks the street, bows down to wash the feet of those who are dusty from the soft, white sand. Are you this one? Who are you? Have you searched within? Have you chosen to shine your Light? Seek within your heart and there you will find the answer.

Reflection

The Creator of Life

There is life force within everything. It expands to embrace the totality of existence. The mind cannot fully comprehend what is beyond the illusion of physical existence. All that exists embraces realms which are beyond the reach of the mind but within the scope of knowingness.

In your knowingness realize the "I AM," that you are and God is. God is the life force of existence. God is the consciousness of the life force of all that exists. Truth is the foundation and fabric of all that exists. Love is the creative life force of existence. God is Love. WHEREVER I AM, GOD IS. Amen.

Illumination

The Tree of Life

From the sanctuary of your silence [7]
Embrace the Light [7]
The source of life [7]

Know from whence your thoughts emerge [7]
Know from whence your feelings emerge [7]
And thereby command your being [5]

Transcend [4] the way of the flesh [3]
With Love [4]
And with Truth [5]

In your knowingness [7]
Realize who you are [6]
Realize your true aspirations [6]
Realize the desires of your Spirit [6]

Embrace your power [5]
With passion to create [2]
With passion [2] to be all that you are [6]

All that you desire is before you [2]
Choose now [5]
And manifest [1]

Amen [7]

Suffer not yourself, for you are a Light, eternally burning and shining. It is your life. Embrace all that you are and shine. Shine from the root to the crown, your totality. It is the purpose of your journey, the journey of the flesh into Light. (The number within each square bracket represents a chakra.)

Illumination

Life

It is all that you are
Here and now
In this very moment.

Stop
Embrace the moment.
Embrace each moment.

From the depths of your silence
Find your essence
And be all that you are
In this very moment.

Illumination

Answers

You are seeking the answer.
You are seeking to fill an emptiness.
Your very being is reaching to the heavens.

Who am I?
What is my purpose?
How do I fulfill my purpose?

Here is the answer.

You seek yourself
Your essence.
You seek that place within where you are all that you are.
You seek the "I AM."

You seek to find that one within.
To manifest that one.

To manifest all that you are.
Sprit and flesh as one.

To be
Love
Truth
Joy

The totality of life.

Lesson 04

On Being

Take the time to know yourself.
To know your heart.
To know your Spirit.
To know your feelings.
Your aspirations.
Your hopes
Your very essence.

Fear not.

Manifest who you are.
Manifest all that you are.

It is your true purpose
To be all that you are.
Amen.

Lesson 05

Sharing

We are all that we are.

You are student.
And I am student.
And as such we are one.

You are teacher.
And I am teacher.
And in such we are one.

We are one
In Spirit
In Truth
In Love
In Life
In God.

We seek to grow manifesting all that we are.

Transcending this reality
Embracing all that is Light
Journeying to that place where all life is one.
Amen.

Illumination

Joy

I seek joy.
I choose joy.
I choose a path that creates joy.

It is my quest in life.
It is my guide.
It is the way.
It is the Truth.
It is the blossom of Love.

My Spirit is Love.
My Spirit is Truth.
My Spirit is my desires made manifest.
My Spirit is my feelings.
My Spirit is joy.

Love for self is joy.
Manifesting Spirit is joy.

Thus
Joy I choose
In each moment.

Meditation

I Am

I am guided by my Spirit.
I am all that I am.
I am Truth.

I am Spirit who embraces the flesh.
I am as I choose.
I am as I create.

I am Love.

Close your eyes and feel. It is who you are. What you feel is the essence of your Spirit. Go beyond the perceptions of the mind and realize what lies beneath. It is the source of Love. It is the source of Truth. You are Love and you are Truth. Embrace this in your meditations. You seek your essence, your true self. Fear not, for you are all that you are. The mind is a vehicle of the body and a tool of the Spirit. Embrace its power to build the life that you choose, one defined by your Spirit, one that is founded upon Truth and Love and become all that you are. Fear not, for you are perfect. Spirit is perfect. Love is perfect. Truth is perfect; thus, you are perfect for your essence is Love and Truth. Choose to embrace all that you are and in so doing, live. It is your life to choose. It is your free will. Where you are is a result of your free will; therefore, let your heart guide you to the place of bliss. Your heart knows the answer, for within your heart speaks with the voice of your Spirit, silently and gently. Walk in patience. Listen in patience. Create in patience. Love in patience. It is with patience that you will possess the blessings of your Spirit. Close your eyes and allow Love to embalm your mind and body. It is the elixir of the Spirit and a transforming power that will unite Spirit and flesh as one.

Chapter Two

Holy Is Your Name

Introduction

You are not one but two, flesh and Spirit. You are the sum of all your sojourns, each with a name given to the flesh. In Spirit, you are the bush that burns from the very root of your being to the crown, an everlasting flame that will not extinguish, yet will not consume you, for it is the source and fountain of your life.

It is a holy presence seen only with your inner eyes. Approach cleansed in body and mind. As you approach this presence, you will find the one known as the "I AM." Know that you are the "I AM." You are the one who you seek. Meditate upon these words and you will travel to the foundation of Truth. You will find answers to questions that emerge from the depths of your being. In this place, the yearning of the Spirit ends. It is the root and source of your power.

To seek the "I AM" is to seek the true self. To seek the "I AM" is to look for the one you were in the beginning, at your birth into Light. To each a name was given in the beginning. It is a name known only by your Spirit, and to be uttered only by Spirit. To seek this one, the "I AM" is the journey into Light.

The Process of Transformation

Where Do I Start?

All answers are held within the palms of Spirit and offered in Love to the consciousness of the seeker. Seek diligently, with humility and patience, as you meditate. Go into the place of silence, physically, mentally and spiritually. Truth will emerge as a Light shining upon the path of transformation. It is a Light that quickens the mind. It is a Light that awakens the body and shines from the Spirit upon the flesh. It is the emergence of the "I AM."

As you think, as you feel, as you choose, as you create, it is a transforming flame that burns from within that seeks to end the dichotomy of flesh and Spirit. As it was in the beginning, so shall it be, here and now as echoed from a time past as seen in the Emerald Tablet of Hermes: "As above, so [shall it be] below," and also from the words of the Nazarene Master: "Thy will be done on earth, as it is in heaven."

As you mediate, seek the flame of Spirit as it was in the beginning, the one that is above, in the heaven of your totality. Seek out the secret name of the Spirit. Choose to let this Light shine, flowing from every cell of your being, every organ, every chakra. Embrace the power to manifest physically the desires of your very own spirit, creating heaven here on Earth.

From the time of your birth into Light, you have had a multitude of sojourns into physicality when the flesh overshadowed the Spirit in a dual existence. Spirit once again seeks to shine through flesh with harmony and oneness. Your Spirit is kind, gentle and patient. Spirit will not overshadow your free will but await your choice.

You exist within a framework engineered by Spirit where you can make choices that manifest your oneness. It is an environment that presents situations which release emotions that awaken cellular memory, triggering patterns from past sojourns. These situations are the opportunities to choose differently, dissolving shadows and blockages created in the past, allowing the transforming Light of the Spirit to shine through the flesh, in harmony and oneness. The enlightened one is guided solely by the Light of the Spirit, the "I AM." The enlightened one manifests physical life in oneness with the "I AM."

Awaken to the voice of the "I AM" and shine with Love and Truth in all your thoughts, words and actions. Know from the very depth of your being that you are the "I AM." With choice, once again you will manifest in oneness the Light which you shine from within.

Truth

Truth is the yarn in the fabric of your being. It is the building block of life. It is the substance of Spirit. The innate desire to manifest Truth emerges from within. It is the voice of your Spirit calling you home. Manifesting Truth ends the dichotomy of flesh and Spirit. In all situations, it is Spirit which offers Truth, and you have the choice and power to recognize this Truth and respond to life as Spirit.

The mind reacts with fear. One of the prime directives of the mind is to ensure survival of the flesh, using extreme measures to maintain its continued existence. The mind will guide you to run and hide from a wild lion or any physical danger.

The mind resists emotional change and employs fear to create boundaries, which limits the opportunities for change. Meeting new people can offer professional or personal opportunities. However, inaction due to the fear of feeling embarrassed or awkward can keep those doors closed.

Reason, whether scientific or otherwise, is also employed by the mind as a tool, which limits opportunities for change. The mind will therefore choose to remain in a familiar environment, and not venture beyond the boundaries of its own comfort zone.

In the journey of life, there is always a choice between flesh and Spirit. If you yield to the way of the mind, you give the mind power over the Spirit. Fear then eclipses the Spirit and becomes the architect of your life.

Consider the eagle. In her wisdom, she tosses her babe from high upon a cliff. Soon the little one learns to spread its wings and soar above the clouds. In its innocence, unimpeded by fear, the eaglet learns how to transcend its perceived limitations and fly free. Hidden behind the protections and boundaries established by the mind, Spirit is seeking to emerge and fly free. Listen to the voice of Truth that shines from within. Learn the lesson of the eagle. It takes trust to accept the guidance offered by Spirit. It takes courage to transcend the way of the mind. You have the power to choose the way of Truth. You need to trust your own Spirit and take that leap of faith. It is the enlightened one who chooses the way of Truth and soars high above the clouds, with the angels.

Spirit Eyes
Out of the midst of the darkness, Light emerges. It is Spirit that shines from beyond upon the flesh. You are Spirit first, a Light, reaching from the depths of eternity, here in the physical realm. It is your Spirit that is here, experiencing the physical world.

The eyes of the Spirit see all and embrace totality. In meditation, your consciousness expands to embrace the Spirit. You become conscious of what the Spirit sees. You become aware of the totality of existence. Truth becomes an open book upon which you gaze. You see what Spirit sees.

Each moment of your existence is defined by your free will to choose. Choice guided by the Light of the Spirit defines your reality. Look upon life with singularity, allowing only the Light of Spirit to shine through your eyes. Recall the words of the Nazarene Master: "The light of the body is the eye: if therefore thine eye be single; thy whole body shall be full of light." You can find this in the Book of Matthew, chapter 6, verse 22.

Intuition
Intuition is a source of guidance offered by Spirit. Your Spirit reaches out to you with Love and Truth, shining a Light onto your consciousness that you may see, hear, feel what is beyond the flesh. It is an inner knowing that is beyond reason, offered in the area of your sixth chakra.

Retreat often to reflect. Listen for the voice of the Spirit that speaks through your intuition. Listen to the voice of the Spirit that speaks through your feelings. Spirit is ever present, reaching out to you, knocking at the door of your consciousness. As you move through life, listen for this guidance. Know that you are never alone.

When you go into meditation, expand your consciousness to embrace Spirit. Open your eyes and gaze upon Truth offered by Spirit. Become cognizant of all your inner senses. Always be prepared to receive this guidance. Always be prepared to respond to challenges with swiftness, employing patience, humility, Love and Truth.

Seeing with the eyes of Spirit is your birthright and a natural function of the totality of your being. Embrace your birthright. Embrace all that Spirit offers. Listen and you will feel the music of Spirit within your heart. Dance to the music. Feel the music of the spheres reverberate within your being. Know that your physicality is an instrument of Spirit. Allow Spirit to play this instrument. It is your choice. Choose this and your life will be transformed. The totality of your being will resonate with life and vibrate with a harmony of joy. Take the time to meditate upon this chakra and dance with joy as you journey onward and upward into Light.

Sixth Chakra Meditation

The purpose of this meditation is to harmonize body, mind and Spirit to expand the energy from the area of the sixth chakra. The aura this energy radiates is a brilliant indigo which flows down to the area of the fourth and second chakras. As you meditate, focus on the area of the sixth chakra. The symbol to hold in your mind is "name," which corresponds with the pineal gland, located in the middle of the brain.

In this meditation, you will gain an awareness of the energies that impact upon your consciousness. You will realize that you are not one but many. There are many layers that encompass and can overshadow the Spirit. You have travelled long and far, and have lived many different and unique lives, each with a unique name. Your mind will wander along the meandering pathways of the past, and old personalities will emerge, seeking to embrace your consciousness. As you meditate, step aside and observe this process. Observe how patterns, which do not serve Spirit, embrace the consciousness. With Love and patience, acknowledge these mental states, which are like footsteps of the past, and ask them gently to leave. They can step aside. They can observe but can no longer have control of your being. As these layers are peeled away one at a time, your true essence emerges, and you gain the insight and awareness of the <u>one</u> you truly are. Your being is filled with joy.

A name was given to this one in the beginning, at the time of your inception into reality. It is a name which represents your true essence, a being of Light. It is the image of the Creator of life that you hold within. This is the sacred place, the consciousness, which you seek to embrace in this phase of your meditation.

As you meditate, allow the energy from the area of the sixth chakra to expand. Like an overflowing cup, allow it to spill over, filling your entire being with Light, touching every cell and organ of your being, awakening and strengthening each energy centre.

Your entire being will shine, illuminated, a tree of Light. You shine from the root to the crown, expanding and flowing beyond the physical realm. You shine so brilliantly you feel like the sun, emanating a warm and transforming energy.

As you breathe, let your energy grow and expand, reaching out, touching, healing, awakening, transforming as it unites as one with the all-embracing Light of creation. Amen.

Walk on Water Meditation

Take time to relax and pray. Seek guidance and protection as you prepare to enter the silence of meditation.

Take a deep and gentle breath, and as you slowly exhale, relax. Become part of the Mother Earth once more. Allow her to sustain your body wherever you are as you find a place to sit and become comfortable.

Take a deep and gentle breath, and as you slowly exhale, relax. From the soles of your feet to the crown of your head, relax every muscle.

As you relax, allow the pull from Mother Earth [gravity] to hold your body in a position of balance. Feel her gentle, sustaining force beneath you, cradling you.

Take a deep and gentle breath, and as you slowly exhale, relax. Relax so deeply that you can feel her touch. Find that place of balance so that she gently holds you, as you relax and prepare to go deep into meditation.

Take a deep and gentle breath, and as you slowly exhale, relax. With each breath that you take, relax. You are like a flower, ready to bloom, burst into golden Light. Go within and feel this part of your being. Feel the connection with the earth beneath you and her gentle, nurturing energy rise up to embrace and nourish you.

Consider a tree, planted deep within the earth, in perfect balance, holding strong against the wind and rain. Like the tree, you are in oneness with the earth beneath you. Realize that you are being cradled, supported in perfect balance.

Take a deep and gentle breath, and as you slowly exhale, relax. Give yourself over to her by allowing her to cradle your body in a cushion of her energy. Like a child, entrust yourself to her fully, for she is the Mother Earth, sustaining all physical life, and you.

Let your body rest. Rest so deeply, that you [your Spirit] can now prepare to take leave and fly free.

Take a deep and gentle breath, and as you slowly exhale, relax. With each breath, relax. Like a flower, let your energy bloom and burst into sparkling and tingling Light.

Feel the freedom. Know that this is the way you were in the beginning. Before time existed, you were Spirit and Light. You walked in freedom. The flesh was just a simple choice. It was a simple choice to walk upon this realm clothed in flesh, and it was a simple choice to shed your clothing and return to the realms beyond.

Know that you have walked as Spirit.
Go within and remember.
Go deep within and remember.
Go deeper and remember.
Remember.

Follow the pathway of Love to that place within where you will find the one you truly are.

Go within and feel.
Feel the Truth within.
Feel the foundation of reality, the foundation of your being.
Feel your essence.
Find this place of purity that is within your being.
Feel that spark within and you are one with God.

Within this energy, you will be guided.
With this guidance, you will find the way.
Here you will find the purity and wonder of life.

Fear not. Have faith and courage. Feel the Light within you. You are a flower of Light.

And what is faith? Know that faith is the strength you hold within, that there is Truth and Light and life beyond the realm of the physical senses.

So now, prepare to take leave, to fly away to a place that is paradise. Prepare to journey to a place of your choosing, your favourite place, your sanctuary, indeed your golden Ashram. See the beauty of this place that is surrounded by still waters, lush vegetation and sweet singing birds.

Embrace that part of your being that is Spirit, and as your consciousness expands, fly free. Go to that sacred place on high where there is only beauty and joy. Journey now to the water's edge, and there, sit and contemplate. Feel the wind, the clouds and the tingling touch of Light upon your face. Feel the freedom of being in Spirit where all things are possible.

Go now, walk upon the surface of the silvery water. Walk across to the other side.

There on the other side, you will see your sanctuary, your golden Ashram that you have created. It awaits you. Open the door and enter. Within the Ashram, you are greeted by angels.

Walk upon the glistening marble passageway. Feel the presence of those who have come to welcome you, loved ones who have gone before are here to embrace you.

As you continue your journey inward, beyond is a room filled with Light. You know that there you must go.

Angels greet you as you enter. Within this room, you behold a sphere, glistening with a rainbow of Light, pouring down upon the jewelled walls.

You bathe in this Light. Every cell of your being is awakened. Each cell responds to different colours shining from the chorus of jewels, and you shine. Every cell of your body shines with purity and beauty.

Once again, you remember who you are. You remember your "name," the one given to you at birth, when you were born as Spirit.

You remember all that you are and have been. Your heart awakens. Your Spirit awakens. You resonate with the totality of Truth. You resonate with unconditional Love and acceptance.

In the middle of this room, there is a circle upon the floor made of one brilliant ruby. Above, a white Light is shining down upon the ruby. You know that you must sit in the circle. It feels soft, comfortable and warm. As you sit in that special place, it is as the sunrise. It is as a thousand suns rising before you, to bathe you in gold and crimson and every colour of the rainbow. You can feel the Light upon the surface of every cell within your being.

Each cell vibrates. Each cell awakens and dances in merriment with the Light that feels like the stars and moon, a celebration of the wonders of this magnificent existence. The Light permeates your being, dissolving your mind and all you can feel is your Spirit as the angels join in the dance.

Feel the energy within. Feel your power. Feel the transformation within. Shine. Feel the warmth and glory of the Light. Become one with the Light. Everything around you is Light. You are surrounded by Light.

You can feel the energy of the angels. You can feel their Love, peace and Truth permeate your being. Your inner eye opens and you can see and feel the Love that surrounds you, caressing every cell of your being. You become Light. The angels reveal themselves to you as Light, in their true state of Spirit Light. You become one in Light.

You are embraced by the Love that they outpour upon you. Everything and nothing exists. All is Love and Light. You have become one with all, embraced by the Light. You realize all that you are. You awaken to the past. You awaken to the future. You become one with the Truth.

As you contemplate, you understand and remember that you have journeyed. You are here in Spirit and must soon return to the earth school.

So, take time now and fully embrace all, for soon you will bid goodbye. Soon you must return.

Embraced by the Light, clothed in Love, receive of the Light and Love that fills this place.

Take this time to gather strength and courage to move forward in life, empowered and guided by the Light.

[Pause]

And it is now time to return. It is time to journey along the marble pathway and bid goodbye to your loved ones. Bid goodbye to the angels. If you choose, accept their invitation to return.

Walk now across the silvery water, to the other side.

Take flight in Spirit, across the mountain, to that distant planet you call Earth, and return to that place from where you journeyed to your physicality.

[Pause]

Breathe gently but deeply, and slowly re-awaken to the consciousness of your physical body, held gently in the arms of Mother Earth.

Give thanks to the earth. Take a gentle breath, and as you awaken, become fully conscious of all that you received.

Once again, you are ready to continue your journey here in this realm, enlightened, embraced fully by Love and Light, as Spirit clothed in flesh.

You are ready to walk onward with Truth. You are ready to walk onward with the new realization gained within your golden Ashram.

With the blessings from the Creators of life, you are now ready to continue your journey here in your earth home, your physicality and the consciousness of your reality.

Be here and now, awakened and fully alert, blessed by all that you have received, as you embark on a new journey onward and upward into Light. Amen.

Prayer

I give thanks for all that I have received. I give thanks for my sanctuary. I give thanks to the angels. I give thanks to the Creator of all life. I give thanks for the blessing of Light that embraces my life with Love and Truth.

I pray for the strength and courage to choose the way of Light in all my thoughts and actions. I pray that this blessing will transform my life that I may walk onward and upward, embraced by the Light, now and always. Amen.

Lesson 06

One Who Seeks to Emerge

There is one within, seeking to emerge. It is one who is patient, kind and gentle, knowing only Love and Truth. It is one who accepts your will and patiently awaits your choice.

Will you choose freedom? Escape the dungeons of a mind submerged beneath fear and dogma? Is it time to travel the road of Truth, manifesting only the Love that brings freedom from entrapment within the confines of the flesh?

You are Spirit. You have always been Spirit. You are the one who waits patiently for the choice to be all that you are. You are the one who seeks to emerge. Arise; take up your bed and walk, onward and upward into the Light of life.

You are Light. Be all that you are.

Lesson 07

Your Name

What Is in a Name?
Why is there so much emphasis on name? Why is there so much concern regarding the selection of children's names? In Truth, there is great power held within a name.

When a child enters physical existence, a spark of eternal Light clothed in flesh that has manifested, the mirror of this reality reflects all that it is. The power of the name lies herein, as seen in this mirror.

Exercise
In exploring the purpose and great power held within a name, here is an exercise you can try. Choose a new name for yourself. Let the name represent someone who has achieved your very highest aspirations, physically, spiritually and mentally. It cannot be the name of anyone you know. The name represents an image held within your consciousness of your highest ideals. It must be unique, simply because you are unique. Select a name that you feel most comfortable with, one that you can cherish always.

This is an exercise that deserves much time and attention. It is a wonderful opportunity to embrace your hidden power. It is an opportunity to realize all that you are.

Using Your Name in Meditation
Choose to awaken the one who your secret name represents. You can learn how to emulate his or her ways. In meditation, you can gain the courage, strength and power needed to walk in his or her footsteps. Realize that if you choose, you CAN become as this one. You can manifest such aspirations.

Meditation will help you emulate the secret one. It will help you manifest this one with your thoughts, deeds and entire being, in all your daily activities. Your meditation will help you embrace the strength and courage that is needed.

Love and Acceptance
As you walk the path of this secret one, be prepared to encounter many challenges. It is an exercise which will help you to see the differences between yourself and the one you aspire to be. If you so choose, this knowledge will guide you to the door to self-acceptance, the pathway of transformation. Realize that the greatest warriors face this battle, and it could happen to you. Prepare to fight for your very life, indeed for your Spirit. Arm yourself with Truth, and with the deepest Love and acceptance which transcends the boundaries of conditions or expectations.

On this path, realize that you are a Light warrior. Each battle brings greater strength. With each step, your challenges will become even greater. The warrior Spirit is never defeated. There are many battles in the war for oneness with Spirit. The war will not end until Spirit is victorious.

Remember that with each choice, each battle, each victory, there are opportunities to gain lessons and enlighten your being.

As you grow in wisdom, you will learn how to find acceptance in all things. What you may perceive as failure in the flesh may be a great victory for Spirit. Wisdom teaches that the perception of failure offers two lessons: acceptance of self and the opportunity to travel further, seeking hidden Truth. Realize that the path of the Spirit is blessed with the Light of the Creator of life.

Take Not the Name of God in Vain.
When you show honour and respect for the name you choose for God, you are honouring and respecting all that is symbolized by your perception of God. You are honouring the Love and Truth that is God. Take not your own "name" in vain, the secret one that you have chosen, for it honours and respects all that is represented

by the highest aspirations of your own being.

All that you are is symbolized by your name. Your Love, your Truth and your word are not only symbols, but the very essence of your being.

You are much like a jewel. When you give your word, it is a facet of your being. When you promise, it is a facet of your being. When you Love, it is a facet of your being. When you choose the virtues of your Spirit such as peace, patience, kindness, charity, honesty, etc., all are facets of your being. Your name is a representation of your essence, the energy held within this jewel, which you are. Your essence can be viewed as the sparkling Light that emerges from this jewel. Remember that your Light is a spark of the eternal that you call God. Take not the name of God in vain, and do likewise for your own self, take not your own name in vain.

Earth
Earth is much like a chest filled with amazing treasures. It is a unique energy that creates clarity, purity, brilliance and beauty. You can embrace this energy and shine. It is your choice, your free will to fill the world with brilliance.

Totems
In the traditions of the native peoples of North America, totem poles have been used for this very purpose. Simply put, each symbol on the pole, which sits one above the other, is synonymous with a name. If you create your own totem pole, there would be symbols that represent your past, present and future. The symbol at the top represents your highest aspiration, one that has achieved all your goals and can fly free from the limitations of this physical realm. The symbol that sits at the top, which represents all that you are, will have wings. It is synonymous with your secret name.

You can create your own totem pole. It does not have to be several storeys high. It can simply be an ornament that you wear around the neck, which would represent past, present and future, and serve as a reminder of your own aspirations, your personal journey onward and upward into Light. It is your return journey home.

Sharing Your Name
When you share your name, let your voice convey the power it holds. Be cognizant of all the facets of your being.

> I am Love.
> I am Truth.
> I am strong.
> I am courageous.
> I am my word.
> I am a being of Light.
> I am all that I am.

When you give your name, speak your sacred name in silence, too, knowing the facets of all that you aspire to become. I am all that I am, and I will be all that I will be. Herein lies the hidden Truth of your name. Be blessed by the power of your name as you journey onward and upward into Light. Amen.

Illumination

The Word Made Flesh

When I speak
It is the voice of Love.
It is the voice of Truth.
It is the voice of my Spirit.

The word is my Spirit.
The word manifests all that I am.
The word is Spirit manifest.

I am the word
The living word
The word made flesh.

Meditation

The True Teacher

Hear to the voice of your Spirit as it speaks to your heart: "Listen to the voice of Truth that speaks from within. There you will find guidance to the Light you seek. To accept Truth offered by another is to accept their control. A true teacher guides you to find the voice of your own Spirit. Follow the guidance of your Spirit and you will find the door to the Light."

There are many who have come your way, which you describe as teachers. Those who have embraced physical life so completely, far beyond what is considered "normal," that they become deified by society. If you examine their way of being, you will find patterns you also can follow or lessons for living. When you manifest your Spirit so completely that your life can be emulated as an example of Love and Truth, you have achieved the state the ancients called "teacher." The one who walked in Nazareth was such a teacher. He embraced the essence of life, the source of Love and Truth so completely, and it is for this he was called "teacher." Furthermore, the mastery of physical life was so complete that he was called "Master."

When you are on a path of self-fulfilment, you can fill yourself with so much Love that you have excess to share. In so doing you can be of benefit not only to yourself, but also to all those around you, to the entire planet and all of existence. Your state of being is intrinsic to all existence. All are connected in many different ways. When you are on a path of self-fulfilment, your life is defined by the deepest desires of your Spirit. Realize that your Spirit is defined by joy. The state of spiritual joy is called nirvana or bliss. The pattern of your life becomes an example, which others will seek after you exhibit the state of true joy.

Lesson 08

The Journey Back

First there was nothing. Then there was Love and Truth. Out of Love and Truth an idea was born. The idea took flight and manifested in this, the physical realm.

You are Love, formed out of Truth. Your power is Love. You have the free will to manifest your power. Out of this free will was born choice. It was the power to choose which manifested an idea which took breath in the physical realm. Out of this power, you created your life as it is. It is this power to choose that will create your future.

Your physicality responds when you exercise your power to choose. The power travels in Light from the seventh chakra to the first where Spirit and cells unite as one. As the Light travels, it ignites each energy centre along the way. It is this fire, which is your life, burning with unique colour and purpose within your being.

The blueprint of Love and Truth emanates from the sixth chakra. The will to manifest this blueprint emerges from the fifth. The heart is the doorway of Love, which holds the power to temper all your activities, if it is your choice. The third chakra is the doorway to the past and holds the Truth regarding the purpose for your sojourns into physicality. The second chakra is the doorway of duality where you choose either the way of Spirit or to aggrandize the flesh. The energy that governs the uniting of Spirit and flesh emerges from the first chakra.

There is balance when the energy centres vibrate in harmony with each other to fulfill one purpose. Remember that choice is the power of your Spirit that resulted in your manifestation into physicality. It is choice that will take you onward and upward on the return journey into Light. Amen.

Lesson 09

"I Am That I Am"

You are the "I AM." Realize this. You are a rock, unchangeable and unmoveable. You are planted firmly in Truth and fed by a fountain of Love. It is your birthright. All that you are is contained within your being, here and now, in this very moment. The world around you may fall away, but you will remain, all that you are, unto eternity.

You have power over life. You have power to choose, manifest, change and be all that you are. It is your free will.

The summation of the "Prayer to Our Father" can be interpreted as "I AM THAT I AM" from Exodus, chapter 3, verse 14 of the King James Version of the Bible. How is this so? The prayer shows how to recognize your essence, your Spirit, your birth Light, your "name," the "I AM." It shows how to transcend all that you have embraced through your sojourns, that part of your being that is ego, and once again through choice and free will, embrace all that you are, the "I AM." You can speak the words within your heart in the silence of meditation, "I AM THAT I AM." Amen.

Lesson 10

Shining Forth

When you take time to contemplate, seeking the Truth of your being [sixth chakra], you understand that the teachers and masters of ancient times (ancients) have taught how to become aware of the Light which you emanate.

As children in a distant corner of creation, it is easy to feel isolated and confused by the challenges that you face, awakening a desire to embark upon a new journey seeking Truth.

The ancients have revealed that there is a place, a consciousness that offers Truth. The ancients have revealed that emanating brilliant colours is an intrinsic part of your being. Your new journey will lead you to that place where you become a perfect rainbow, shining with brilliance like a star in the distant sky, a place of eternal joy.

Which colours would you like to emanate? How do you charge your batteries so you shine more brilliantly? The answers all lie within.

As Light beings, it is your purpose here in this realm to shine, to make existence a brighter place. By being all that you are, your entire being becomes filled with Light.

What colours will you choose to emanate in brilliance? It is yours to command. It is all within the realm of your choice.

During meditation, examine your affirmations and the choices they offer. Contemplate the nature of the Light that each choice will manifest. Make choices that manifest your brilliance.

Whenever you see a rainbow, let it be a reminder that you are a rainbow of Light. Your aura shines with a rainbow of colours. You are an emissary of Light. Like the rainbow, realize that your manifestation in this realm is multifaceted. Know that within, you are the brilliance of all the colours of the rainbow.

Let your inner Light so shine, brightening your path, and the paths of all that you seek. Shine with brilliance, thereby fulfilling the task of adding more and more Light to existence.

Illumination

Feel the Spirit

Feel that Spirit within.
Feel the Truth and the Love.
Feel the Light.

Shining

Enlightened

On the journey home.

Prayer of Love and Light

I give thanks that I can share in the Love and Light which flows from the Creator of life. I give thanks that all may grow in this Love and Light. I pray that my eyes may be opened by the Light of the Creator of life so I may see the Truth which leads to the totality of my being. I pray that I may gain the understanding to embrace all that I am.

I pray that the angels walk with me, talk with me and guide me so I may find my true purpose. I pray that I grow in wisdom to accept all that I am, regardless of condition or expectation. I pray that the Light of creation shines upon the path before me as I fulfill my purpose here in this realm.

The greatest Love in existence is the Light, which the Creator of life shares. Help me to understand and embrace this Love in my daily existence that I may grow and shine with brilliance.

I give thanks for life, and for the all the opportunities that it offers. I give thanks for Truth and Love, and the Light, which shines in all peoples. Help me the see this Light and live in its glory and blessing. Offer me the blessing that I may nurture this Light, brightening life for all in this realm and beyond.

I seek the protection and guidance of the Creator of life in all that I do and say. Walk with me now and with each step I take, on my journey onward and upward into Light. Amen.

Morning Prayer

I give thanks for this new day. I give thanks for the Light at dawn. I give thanks for the Light that inspires me to share the Love, peace, kindness, hope and joy that each new day offers.

I give thanks for the Light, which fills my heart, mind and body, reaching to the depths of my being. I ask that the Light surround and protect me now and in the days to come.

I ask the angels to travel upon the wings of Light and stand with me, to protect, guard and guide me. I ask the angels to show me the way, which leads to the fulfillment of my Spirit. I ask the angels to intervene in my life, clearing the pathway before me.

I ask for the guidance of the Creator in all that I do, so I may be inspired to follow the pathway of Truth and Love. I ask for the strength and courage to face all the trials that come my way, that I may be victorious in the battle for Love, Truth and all the virtues of life.

I ask for guidance that I may understand the secrets of life, which lead to the Truth, opening the door to eternal Light. Help me to gather wisdom to see the Truth, which is before me, and grant me the strength and courage to choose the pathway of Love and Truth, each day and each moment that I may journey onward and upward into Light. Amen.

Prayer of Light

I give thanks for Light that is life. I give thanks for the harmony it brings to my life. I give thanks for the power to radiate a rainbow of Love and Light, as I journey along the path of life. Amen.

Lesson 11

Love and Light

To receive guidance from the Spiritual realm is a wonderful experience. It is what you seek to protect and guide you in each moment, and as you face everyday challenges.

There is a story of a young man who sought inner peace and made his way to the lake where he could find a serene place to meditate. It may remind you of the challenges that unexpectedly come your way. After sitting beside the calm waters, contemplating life, free of the disturbances from cars and people, he felt connected with nature and all that was around him. As the peace and calm overtook him, he was attracted to the water, and after meditating, he decided to swim. Unprepared and quite alone, robed only in his birthday suit, he lost himself in the still and clear water. Time went by swiftly. It was such a glorious day.

Later, several wonderful ladies appeared in the distance. The young man became frantic as they approached, for he realized that they were between him and his clothes. Still far away, he emerged from the water and covered himself with an old bucket, not noticing that the bottom was missing.

Why do you find yourself in such predicaments, and how do you avoid them? If you pray each day with deep conviction, will this offer protection? If you seek guidance from the realms beyond, will this bring protection? If you become an instrument of Love and Truth, offering services to all of humanity, will this bring the desired protection?

As you travel the road of life seeking protection, many questions gnaw from within.

(a) Why do I face such difficult challenges?
(b) What is my purpose here in the physical realm?
(c) What is the purpose of existence?
(d) What is Light?
(e) What is Love?
(f) What is Truth?
(g) As you wander the meandering road of life, and you receive the greeting "Love and Light," what does it mean?
(h) When you pray for world peace, will it ever happen?
(i) Will the road ever lead to a place of Love and Truth and indeed the elusive state of enlightenment?

You must realize that the challenges you face each day, regardless how simple or complex, will help open a door. What you are today is the result of the challenges of yesterday. The challenges of today will define your tomorrow.

Here is a hypothetical situation. Suppose you are a bank manager, and you erroneously receive a million dollars, but you are the only one who knows about it. What would you do? Would you allow the bank to keep the money?

Here is another hypothetical situation. Suppose YOU received one million dollars due to an error. You know to whom it belongs, but you and only you know of this. What would you do?

Or suppose you are the only other person who knows about the million dollars. Your close friend is now in possession of the loot, in cash. Your friend is not sharing it, but you know all the details. What would you do?

In the struggles of today's society, many dream of wealth! What are you prepared to do for this wealth? How would you face these hypothetical situations? How do you face the situations which come your way when you least expect them? What is your responsibility to society, yourself and the Truth? What is the price of your integrity? Ponder these questions, seeking peace within. Even the simple choices of today will define not only your tomorrow, but also what you take with you beyond this realm into eternity. Your choices are the defining factor of your totality, here and beyond.

Here are some thoughts to consider. There are many changes on the crust of the Earth, society, belief systems, technology, governments and religions across the globe. What is your role in all this? What will be the challenges of a new tomorrow? Within your heart, do you feel that there will there be a place for peace, Love, harmony and creativity? What must you do in your little corner of the world, and how will you do it?

Seeking answers is a slow and arduous journey. Much like sore muscles that find comfort and joy after a workout, in a greater sense, you gain divine joy as you choose to follow the path of Love and Truth. The process of choosing can be a difficult and an agonizing challenge.

On this journey, it is Love and Truth that becomes your very existence. Your life is embraced by these virtues as they form a crucible of the Spirit. Nothing matters but the desires of the Spirit, which is Love and Truth. A million dollars will hold no value, for money does not feed the spirit, nor offer eternal joy!

Go into meditation knowing that you are Spirit, and find the place within from which Spirit shines. Let your life in the flesh be directed by the Spirit within. Let the Light that Spirit shines from within be a channel of your Love and Truth, embracing all that you touch and connecting all as one.

Realize that you are a being of Light. You are a being of Love. Your Spirit is Love. You are Love. Journey with joy as you embrace Love. Journey with joy as you embrace the Light. Embrace the essence of your Spirit and journey onward and upward into Light.

Illumination

The Journey into Light

Be true to yourself.
Your feelings are a reflection of your Spirit.
The foundation of the Spirit is Truth.
The life of the Spirit is Love.

To manifest your feelings is the deep desire of the Spirit.
It is the path of life.
The journey onward and upward into Light.
Amen.

Illumination

Validity

No less
No more
Equal to all

My thoughts
My feelings
My place
All valid

My heart
My Truth
My word
All valid

The Light I shine
All that I am
My totality
All valid

In each moment
I validate myself
Being no less
Being no more
Being equal to all
Being all that I am

It is about being who you are and all that you are despite the circumstances or situations you encounter. Examine your past and you will see the lessons and the patterns that opened doors to the Light. Seek this in meditation, remembering always that the pattern embraces Love, Light and joy that emerge from the heart. Embrace this pattern. There is nothing more important.

Reflection

Choose Thou

Today you are one
But tomorrow you are gone.

Are you truly gone?
For life continues
In the beyond.

As you rise above
And travel that road of Truth
You behold a glorious kingdom
One held in the palm of your hands
A place filled with Light.

A mighty creation
A mighty choice.

Choose thou
And live.

Lesson 12

The Doorway to the Light

You face Truth in all things. No matter how vast the challenge, it is Truth that manifests the purity of life. Truth is the pathway to reality.

The decisions you make define your reality. The decisions of yesterday define your reality today. Your choices in the moment define who you are.

Are your decisions based on the ways of the heart? Are your decisions based on Love? Such choices open the door to the Light.

The greatest challenges you will face are based on Love and Truth. Being victorious will open doorway to the Light. Seek, therefore, a way of being that is based upon Love and Truth. You seek the one who is within, the one you truly are, the one defined by your true "name" as revealed by the sixth chakra meditation.

With Love, build your foundation upon the rock that is Truth. Let your consciousness always be filled with Love and Truth, enlightened and immovable, as you embrace all that you are on your journey through that doorway, onward and upward into Light.

Lesson 13

The Path of Truth

How do you know Truth?
How do you know what is the right path?
How do you know what to choose?

Life is about choosing the path of Truth.
Life is about living this Truth.
Life is about manifesting Truth.

You walk a path of challenge.
You fight battles with Truth.
You fill your heart with Love.

Such is the way of the Spirit.
Such is the Light of life.
Such is your destiny.

Lesson 14

Oneness

It is the mind that navigates your physical life. Have you ever wondered where the mind gets its instructions? Social signals such as anger, fear or jealousy influence the direction of your mind. Your Spirit Light which shines from within also offers Truth which can be applied by the mind. You have free will, which is your power to choose, or you can give away your free will by accepting the control of another's will.

How will you choose to navigate your life? Within the heart of all lies the seed of Love. In meditation, seek this and you are on the path of oneness. Learn the lessons of the Nazarene Master when he shared, "I and the Father are one," in John chapter 10, verse 30 of the King James Version of the Bible.

Lesson 15

The Living Example

Children are a powerhouse of energy, with such potential held within the confines of their being, awaiting a channel of release. Their chakras dance with power. Their endocrine system works with the highest efficiency. How will all this raw energy be manifested? What choices will the children make as they traverse the coming-of-age bridge?

There are many forces, external and internal, which impact the choices of children. There is the Spirit within, the mind and physical desires. Also, there are external forces, such as entities or energies which seek to manifest their will through those who are receptive. The receptive are not always prepared to consciously choose. When new situations arise, they react based on instinct or patterns offered by the mind, patterns created in the past. They may also react based on patterns offered by external sources.

There is a simple answer. Always choose the way of Love and Truth. However, are children prepared to consciously choose in the moment and with each breath? Are they trained in the fine art of discernment and observation? Are children made aware of the power of the will and the freedom it offers? Instead, when situations arise, choices are based on physical desires, peer pressure, church, parents or even government. Television is also a powerhouse of patterns for the impressionable by presenting scenarios which remain in the mind and easily become the chosen direction when future situations and challenges arise.

What is the answer? Children learn by the example of parents, church, government, television and so on. Can a society that is founded solely upon Love and Truth be established? That sounds like utopia. Ask yourself the question: "Is it truly possible?" What is your answer?

You must realize that nothing is impossible. Consider this. How many droplets of water or grains of sand make an ocean? In Truth, there is a number. It can be counted, one grain or one drop at a time. There is a finite number. What may seem impossible is possible if you have the skill and the patience.

If you look at your history, you will see that it took only one person to significantly change the way of thinking and the course of history for all humanity. This happened many times. You can be that one if you so choose. Remember that all things are possible if you are willing to make that choice, one small step, one voice at a time. How many voices make up all of humankind? Stand up and be counted.

Are you willing to manifest the Love and Truth, which emerges from within the depths of your being? Are you willing to be the one you truly are? Are you willing to take steps to manifest your essence? Are you willing to be the living example for tomorrow?

Lesson 16

Knowingness

It is with your knowingness that you embrace all that you are from this moment to the moment of your birth into reality.

Consciousness is the awareness in this very moment of all that is offered by the physical and spiritual senses.

As you grow and embrace the fullness of Spirit, your consciousness expands to embrace all that Spirit embraces. Your knowingness embraces the consciousness of all that is.

Knowingness is the consciousness of Spirit. It is your heart that is the doorway to your knowingness. Listen to the voice of your heart and you will open a door to the depths of your being wherein your knowingness lies.

Reflection

The Voice of the Spirit

What is "creedal slavery"? It is the dogma found in religion, society, families and everywhere. It limits growth beyond its boundaries. It limits the acceptance of Truth and Light.

The desperate search for answers is a challenge all have experienced. Perhaps you have already discovered that answers do not come easily. Often you search and search the libraries, bookstores and the Internet. You seek out favourite authors and gobble them up. The search sometimes seems fruitless, but you never, ever give up. More books, more libraries, more friends, more teachers and the unrelenting search continues, on and on.

You may spend hours or days or weeks or years meditating and contemplating life. Sometimes you search so hard you get lost along the path, forgetting the question you asked and where you started. You get side-tracked. Nonetheless you continue to search because you know you will find an answer. You know that you will know what you are searching for, when you find it.

The desire of your Spirit is to find an answer. For the moment, the question is not important. It will come later. Isn't life interesting? Isn't life so much fun when you can take a moment to step aside to look at yourself? Even if you do know what you are searching for, would it change anything? Would you continue your search for that elusive answer, the answer, for which you do not yet know the question? Although it may feel hopeless at times, it really isn't. Otherwise you would not be here, seeking.

Ancient teachers believed in a journey of continuous progress. For many, it is a promise that there will be fulfillment. It is a promise that there will be answers. It is a promise that joy and eternal happiness are possible and within your reach.

You do not have to believe the ancients. If you take a moment to seek within your own heart, you will discover that the answers speak from the voice of your own Spirit.

It is the great teachers of the past who offered, "Truth lies within." As you explore this, it is important to choose to accept only *your* own Truth, instead of what is provided through external sources.

What have you found in your travels?

It is true that the answers do come. Often they come unexpectedly and in the strangest ways. Interestingly, each answer opens a door to many more questions. You soon realize, however, that it is *the journey* that life offers which leads to the Light, and it is the *experiences* that constitute the journey.

How would you define "progress of the Spirit"? Is it in finding answers? It is in the opening of the door, which allows the Light to shine in. Each challenge you encounter is an opportunity. If you choose to accept the challenge, it becomes an opportunity to face yourself. Victory will allow your Light to shine from within. Each victory is defined as progress.

Perhaps life's lessons can be viewed as a mirror. If you look at each situation carefully, you will see how you responded to your own attitudes and emotions. You will see whether your reactions were based on fear or Love. Try it sometime. You will find it is Truth. As you meditate upon this, you will guided towards success and happiness in your own life.

Here is a story that will perhaps help you put it all into perspective. It is a true story about an old man who spent his whole life in the service of humanity. He worked in the church and was also a teacher. He taught philosophy, and with this, he had brought understanding to many who were seeking. He helped the poor. He raised money for charities. He did all what society expected from a "good" person. His teachers and superiors were very satisfied with his work. Indeed, he felt a certain amount of satisfaction in his achievements. Many loved him.

But he had grown tired. You could see it in his eyes. His thin white hair also revealed how much he had aged. As he lay in the hospital bed and reviewed his life, he knew his days were coming to an end. He marvelled at his journey. A small and gentle smile came upon his face as he recounted the many successes along his path, the people he touched with his teaching and the lives he had changed because of the charity work he established.

He felt that he had fulfilled all that was required of him. Indeed, his ma and pa would have been proud, if they were still alive. This made him feel sad, yet happy. He also had the consolation that society was proud of him. His teachers and colleagues were proud of him and showed great appreciation for his work.

As he lay in bed and pondered, his eyes sparkled as he relived so many joyous moments and felt that he had done a good job. He had done all that was required of him. He was a good son, a good servant, a good teacher and a good leader. He had lived a humble life of service.

Inside, however, he felt emptiness. He felt unhappy. He felt unfulfilled. It brought a tear to his eye. After so many successes throughout his life, he did not know why such a feeling would embrace him, and hold him so strongly.

Answers came to him easily when others sought his council. As he mused, a frown grew upon his face. Though he tried, he could not put his finger on the reason for this emptiness. He could not shake the feeling. As he wondered and contemplated, and looked towards the blue of the sky, his teary eyes became heavy and soon closed with sleep.

While he slept, he had a dream. In this dream, he was in a place of peace and beauty, filled with magnificent Light. Such peace he had not experienced. Such beauty he had not known in his lifetime.

With him was his beloved teacher, his guide, and one who loved him deeply. His teacher spoke.

"My son," the gentle voice came. "I feel your emptiness and your pain. My eyes fill with tears. I know your heart so well, my son.

"And look around me, my son. See, you have many visitors. Your angels are here, as well. They have come to be with you. They have come to comfort you, but as you can see, their eyes are also filled with tears.

"Please know that they have rejoiced in your every success. We all rejoiced with each of your accomplishments. We have been at your side through all of them.

"But as you see, their eyes are now filled with tears. They feel your emptiness and your pain. We all share in your sorrow of your emptiness.

"It is always like this, my son. We feel all that you feel.

"Know this, my son. Your work has brought great happiness to many, both in this realm and in your world.

"The angels near and far have rejoiced and sung songs of joy, because of your achievements. Be glad for this blessing and the happiness you have brought to so many. Be glad in the knowing that you have opened many doors, and many now walk in Light because of the blessings that you have channelled to them. We in this realm rejoice in these wonderful achievements.

"My son, we feel your tears so deeply. We know of your longing and your emptiness. We have spoken to you of this many times, but the voice of your parents, and society and your colleagues and your superiors were much louder and stronger. Our voices are always quiet and gentle. The voice of Love and Truth is always quiet and gentle.

"You, my most dear one, we honour and respect your free will and always accept your choice. We stand with you in Love, regardless of your choice, always.

"You remember the dreams we brought to you at the time of your decision making, in your early years, in your realm? You remember all the wonder and joy that you felt, when you explored your options? I remember seeing the joyous sparkle in your eyes.

"You came here, my son, to be an artist. If you had chosen this, as you had dreamt, and felt so deeply within, it would have brought you the fulfillment and the happiness you now lack. You came to this realm at this time, my son, to show the beauty you hold in your heart, with paint. Your work would have been an inspiration to many, in ways that you have not even imagined. If you seek within, you will find that I speak the Truth of your inner-most desires, locked deeply away, after so many long years.

"Be blessed, my son, in the joy you have brought to so many. Be content with the choices you have made. We embrace you always and stand by your side always with Love and acceptance. We will never judge you.

"Remember always to seek within, and know that we are with you, in dreams and the gentle, small voice which calls to you. Know, my beloved son, that there is always fulfillment and happiness within that voice of the Spirit. Seek and we will always answer."

With this, our dear friend had closed his eyes for the last time.

Lessons come in many different ways. This lesson touched the old man deeply. It was too late for him to find his own true fulfillment, but instead he chose to share his lesson with others, as a guide from the other side of life sharing Love and Truth as the source of joy.

Gather a lesson from our dear friend and choose not to allow your life to be controlled or directed by "creedal slavery." Listen to the voice of Spirit that speaks from within and make choices which bring eternal joy, here, now and in this very moment.

The story of our dear friend did not end. After much contem-plation and consultation with his guides, teachers and angels, and with much gratitude, he did choose to return once again to the physical realm and manifest his desire to be an artist.

Today, many know of the Sistine Chapel frescoes and the works of one called Michelangelo di Lodovico Buonarroti Simoni, the Italian sculptor, painter, architect, and poet.

Reflection

On Dreaming

Your Spirit creates dreams to help you understand life. Dreams are not meant to be taken literally. They bring messages about current situations using symbols and emotions from daily experiences so that what is happening can be viewed from a different perspective. Most often, it is about a situation that is not conducive to your success and happiness. It could be related to a job, school, relationship, spirituality or anything about your life. Dreams are sometimes prophetic in nature.

Recurrent dreams are of particular importance because your Spirit is desperately trying to reach your conscious mind by repeating a message about a situation which is affecting your ability to navigate your life onward and upward into Light. Often each dream would be slightly different, presenting the situation from different perspectives to help with the interpretation.

Dreams do not offer solutions. They show what is happening, and you have the free will to choose a new or different direction in life. Have faith in who you are. It is always best to make choices using integrity and your best wisdom. Let Love and Truth be the foundation of guidance with the objective of personal happiness while not hurting anyone in the process.

The dreamer is always the best one to interpret the dream because of personal and intimate knowledge of feelings about the situation. Everyone is capable to understanding their dreams. Like learning to ride a bicycle or play a musical instrument, it takes perseverance and patience. It takes practice. When you dream, write it down in a journal. During the day, review the dream and the emotions associated with the dream. If you don't see the meaning, try again later. With practice, you will understand and even become an expert.

Life is a journey of challenges that result in learning and growing. It is about understanding who we are, accepting the positive and negative and making new choices that lead to greater success and happiness. It is about challenging yourself to be all that you can be. The greater the challenge, the greater the benefit.

Once you embark on this journey, help will come from many avenues. The dream realm is only one of them.

Lesson 17

I AM

I am Love.
I am Truth.
I am the power of my Spirit.
I am a rock, unchangeable and unmoveable.
I am my word.

I am creative.
I am in command of my being.
I am without fear.
I am accepting.

I am a song.
I am in the wind.
I am the world.

I am a Light that others may see.
I am a teacher by example.

I am joyful for I choose my Spirit.
I am all that I am and will be all that I am.

Reflection

I

How shall I Love me?
I have found the way
To manifest my heart.
The centre of my being.
The one that I truly am.
My true "name."
I
Amen.

Reflection

Focus

The mind seeks to distract and draw you away by taking you along sinuous pathways and avenues. The mind seeks to be in control and will do whatever it can to divert you from your focus, your centre, your essence, your embrace of Spirit.

Be cognizant of mind and Spirit and be ready to command the mind to be quiet, to find yourself, your centre, your Spirit, your place of reflection, the place where hope, Love and Truth emerge, the place where the eyes of Spirit open to embrace all.

Illumination

Emerge

It is I
The I AM
My heart
My name
My word
Truth
Love
Light
Me

Illumination

Realize Who You Are

That you are valid.
That you are beautiful.
That you have purpose.
That you are a being of Truth.
That you are worthy of Love.
That you are a being of Light.

Accept the lessons of your past when you choose, and you will walk the pathway of Light shining from within the heart of your Spirit. Know that you are Love and Truth and that joy is your birthright. Be patient with yourself. Take time to meditate and find your centre. Your life is worth it.

Realize also that wherever you find yourself and in whatever state you find your consciousness, there is always hope in the Light that shines from within. Be committed to yourself. Contemplate daily and open the door to your heart. Listen for the voice of your own Spirit. Let this be your guide. Your very life depends on it. Your life depends on you. You are worth it. You are the only one who can navigate your life along the pathway of Truth to the place of joy and fulfill the desires of the heart.

Awaken each day with a song in your heart. Sing the words of your Spirit and let this vibration resonate in all your works as you journey along life's pathways.

Awaken to the Light of your life and let it be your guide as you journey onward and upward into the heart of your being. Amen.

Reflection

Protect Your Treasures

Embrace all that you are.
Embrace all that is Truth.
Embrace all that is Love.
Embrace your very essence.

These are your eternal treasures.

Guard and protect them
Lest they be snatched away.

Your future depends on it.
Your life depends on it.

Meditation

I See

I see Spirit beside me as my guide.
I see the one I truly am.
I see that I am Truth.

I see the way to live.
I see a new path before me which I choose.
I see the way to create life.

I see the transforming power of Love.
Amen.

Chapter Three
Thy Will Be Done

Live long and prosper. Herein lies the answer to your longevity. Some age gracefully while others fade with time. Take command of your life and embrace the will to choose your own path.

Introduction

When you are unyielding in the way of the Spirit, visible in your aura is a brilliant blue Light shining from the area of the fifth chakra. It is the energy of your steadfast intentions that is glowing.

All the energy centres within your being work in harmony. The eyes of your Spirit see and know the Light of the Creator who offers Love, Truth and guidance. It is the fifth chakra that holds the power to manifest what Spirit sees.

The fifth chakra is connected to the third by way of the heart. When there is balance, they work in unison and energy flows up and down. Emotions that emerge out of the third chakra activate patterns held within cellular memory. Response to emotions may be tempered by the energy of the fourth, and governed by the Truth, which emanates from the fifth.

A beautiful sunrise can bring peace and tranquility, but the weather can change, creating devastating storms which can permanently alter the lives of many. Life is sometimes such a mystery.

What happens in the very next moment can be so profound it can re-define your future. Your reaction to a simple situation can take you in a surprisingly different direction.

You have worked hard to maintain a spiritual persona, but there are situations which can cause it to disappear, and you change into a different person. How do you avoid or transcend such situations, always maintaining your steadfast purpose?

Cellular memory activated by emotions can cause old patterns to emerge. Realize that there is far more depth and dimension to your life than your consciousness allows you to see. All your past incarnations are imbedded deep within as cellular memory. Encountering someone or a situation tied to the past can trigger cellular memory or old patterns. For example, the presence of money, power, food, sex, etc., can stir emotions connected to old patterns, which you instinctively assume without realizing in the moment what is happening.

How do you maintain your spiritual persona when these situations arise? The resurfacing of old patterns offers the opportunity to choose differently. Instead of being blindly controlled by emotions, you can take command of your being by choosing patterns which unify with Spirit. It is an opportunity to face self with Love and acceptance. It is an opportunity to manifest the Truth of the Spirit in all circumstances. It is an opportunity to manifest your word as flesh.

You can maintain your spiritual persona by being vigilant in observing yourself. Use the mind as a tool commanded by Spirit to observe life, your intentions and interactions with others. Observe how you react to their emotions. Observe your own emotions. Become cognizant of emerging triggers. Become aware of whether you are being controlled. Determine if you have given away your will.

Many exist under the influence of the first and second chakras, being controlled by passion or fears associated with survivability. Society is largely based on the fear of lack. Are you being controlled by such social dogma? Are you under the influence of an environment in which society, government, parents, church, friends and family all play a part in how you manifest choice? Is your life based on a legacy of creeds? Many relationships are based on control, whether it is between friends, family or spouses. Often there is one who is dominant, drawing upon the very life energy of another to remain in control. You must realize that to yield to external control is a choice. To give away your free will is a choice.

What happens when controls are lifted? Will you use the newfound freedom for self-aggrandizement? Will you use the opportunity to unfetter Spirit and manifest your purity, your essence, your inner beauty, your Love and Truth?

What happens when controls are added? Will you bow down to unjust laws or the pressures of new social norms or will you honour Spirit and yield not to the ways and creeds of the world?

The process of observation offers the opportunity to choose how to respond. Honouring Spirit is a choice. Manifesting your will is a choice. Manifesting the will of Spirit is a choice. Being in command of your being is a choice. Reflecting Spirit in your word is a choice.

In all things, you have the power to choose [Unless you have given away your free will]. You can offer compassion, acceptance, Love, Truth, charity, kindness, hope and peace to yourself and all others, maintaining your spiritual persona. You have the chance to end the dichotomy between flesh and Spirit, with a path of singularity, which emerges by your command.

Sparkling with Blue
Let Truth be the foundation of all your interactions, thereby maintaining your Spiritual persona unimpeded by anyone or anything. When you speak, enunciate your Truths clearly and forcefully, for they <u>are</u> Truths, which emanate from your Spirit. In so doing, your aura shines with a pure, clear, brilliant Light seen by the eyes of Spirit as blue. Allow the radiance of this energy to brighten your way as you journey upward and onward into the totality of your being.

Imagine a mighty sword that reflects only blue Light, with a blade, strong and sharp, and a handle encrusted with large blue sapphires. Truth is such a sword. As a warrior of Light, you carve your way through life by manifesting Truth with the power and will to create a reality guided by the Spirit. Therefore, let your intentions reflect only the blue Light of Truth.

In meditation, contemplate the following questions:

(a) Are you walking along a path paved with Truth?
(b) How much of your life is directed by your own Spirit?
(c) Do you exercise your free will to manifest what you choose?
(d) What should you do to regain command of your being and manifest the Truth of your Spirit?

Realize that you have the power to maintain the integrity of your Spirit by speaking your Truth. You have the power to be true in all things and with everyone. You have the power to be true to yourself. You have the power to manifest your own will and to be the manifestation of Truth in this realm. Let your word be your Truth. Let your Truth be your word.

As you grow, the power of your sword grows. You have the power of a mighty sword. Pick it up. Keep it at your side at all times. Swing it at will. Stand up for the Truth, which is the fabric of your being. Defend the essence of your Spirit. Manifest your purity and humanity. Maintain the state of your Spirit.

Become aware of the power that you hold. Realize your own potential. Know where you are going. Manifest the life that you choose. As you journey, the flesh may grow weak and fade, but the Spirit will always remain strong with the might to sustain you to the very end. Know the source of your strength. Know the source of your life. Know the source of your health. Know the source of your longevity. The Spirit holds the power to nourish the physicality to maintain its journey onward and upward. Listen and you will hear the words: "Victory will be yours," says your Spirit. Trust in the Spirit by trusting yourself.

Self-Determination

Life is about self-determination through the mastering of your will to manifest Love and Truth within the chaotic encounters of existence. There is much around you that seeks to alter your focus. There are forces which seek to manifest their will through the activities of your chakras. Consider each of the lower three chakras and the challenges they create. Look at the world around you and realize how morals, customs, religion, government, family, friends, television, technology, etc. can manipulate you. There are so many forces that seek control by drawing upon your power. It is the mastering of will that enables you to remain in command of your being, empowering you that you may choose self-determination to navigate your pathway onward and upward into the Light.

Let your meditations become your source of strength, like a rock, unchangeable and unmoveable, on your journey into Light.

Fifth Chakra Meditation

The purpose of this meditation is to harmonize body, mind and Spirit to expand the energy from the area of the fifth chakra. The aura this energy radiates is brilliant blue, which flows down to the area of the fourth and third chakras.

As you meditate, focus on the area of the fifth chakra. The symbol to keep in mind is "will." It is the will to manifest your Truth. The purpose of focusing on this area goes beyond activating the fifth chakra. It relates to the flesh and Spirit working as one. The fifth chakra corresponds with the thyroid gland, located in the throat.

Like a tree which receives sustenance from above and below in a dance of energy that flows up and down manifesting life, so also the system of chakras within your being can be viewed as a tree of life. As you observe the chakras, you become aware that each connects with the other, working in oneness. Energy flows up and down to form such a tree of Light. The golden Light of guidance flows from above, the seventh chakra illuminating your being, guiding you to seek the "one" you truly are [the sixth chakra]. The guidance you receive is manifested through the will of the Spirit, [the fifth chakra]. Realize that the energy is your life.

The three "upper" chakras work in harmony with each other, forming the pattern of life to be manifested in the three below. This Truth, this philosophy, this concept, dates back to ancient times. "As above, so below" was written on the Emerald Tablet of Hermes. Similarly, the Nazarene Master shared: "Thy kingdom come, thy will be done, on earth as it is in heaven."

In this meditation, seek the balance of the upper three chakras and shine with a clear, brilliant, blue Light of Truth. Embrace the power to grow in strength. Remember always that you are in command of your being, if you so choose. It is your free will. What will you choose?

Choose self-determination. Grow strong with the will to determine who you are, now and always. Be prepared to leave the comfort zone of the flesh, which has been established by the mind. You have the power to define a new tomorrow.

Embrace the energy of the fifth chakra to grow strong and shine. Manifest free will and take command of your being to reveal what is above, bringing the kingdom of heaven down to the earth, to your flesh and daily activities, with the power to create your own tomorrow.

You are the manifestation of Love. You are the manifestation of Truth. You are the manifestation of Spirit here in the flesh. It is your purpose to find that place where your Spirit, your Truth, your Love and your flesh are united as one.

Embrace the strength and courage gathered from this meditation so you become empowered in your daily existence, a new being, Spirit as one with the flesh, Spirit in command. Embrace the power to command your own life. Empower yourself to choose Love and Truth in each moment as guided by your Spirit.

Meditation of the Churches

Find a quiet place where you can feel peace and calm. Sit in a comfortable position, whether it is in the forest, beside a river, with a group or in the privacy of your bedroom. With the spine gently erect, close your eyes and relax.

Take a gentle breath and relax as you slowly exhale. Accept Love that is without condition to fill your heart, fully and completely as you breathe. Nourish your mind, body and Spirit with each breath you take.

Nourish your mind with Love. Dissolve all the cares of this realm. Allow the tiredness, the weary want for peace and harmony, any hurt and pain, all distracting energies that you may feel to depart, and allow peace and harmony to encompass your entire being. You are now in command of your mind. You are now in command of your body. Command your being to relax.

Take a gentle breath and as you slowly exhale, relax. You are the master of your being, in command of every muscle. Your mind accepts every command without question or pause.

Take a gentle breath and as you slowly exhale, relax. Feel the essence of your life. Feel the essence of all life. Feel the peace that surrounds you. As peace fills your being, embrace the feeling of calm that is undisturbed by forces, internal and external.

Take a gentle breath and as you slowly exhale, relax. Feel the essence of your life. Feel the essence of all life. Feel the essence of Love. As Love fills your being, embrace the feeling of acceptance without condition or judgment for your life and all that exists.

Take a gentle breath and as you slowly exhale, relax. Feel the essence of your life. Feel the essence of all life. Feel the essence of Truth. As Truth fills your being, embrace the power that Truth commands. Feel this power within you.

As you breathe, relax and feel who you truly are. Realize that you are the embodiment of Love and Truth. Become one with Love. Become one with Truth.

Take a gentle breath and relax. As you slowly exhale, realize that you are a being of Light. Feel the Light within. Feel the Light flowing up and down. Feel the Light touch every cell of your being. You are Light. Embrace the freedom of the Light to fly free. Allow the Light of life to lift you up.

Take a gentle breath, and as you relax be lifted in Spirit. You are a being of Light. Spirit is Light. With Spirit, all things are possible. No longer fettered by the flesh, as the Light you are, fly free, high in the sky.

As you allow your Spirit to be lifted, know that you are not alone, and there is nothing to fear. Know that you are never alone. To fly free of the flesh is natural for your Spirit.

Take a gentle breath and relax. As you slowly exhale, feel the presence of your guides. Feel the presence of your angels. Feel the Love and Light surround and protect you.

As you journey in Light, seek Truth. Know that as you seek Truth, all that offers Truth will embrace you. Let Truth be your guide. Call upon the angels to guide and sustain you. Feel the gentle touch of their wings of Light around you as you are lifted high in the sky.

And the first angel stands forth in a burst of brilliant, clear, glimmering red. Be lifted by the gentle touch of this angel, feel that sense of completeness and contentment. You desire nothing. Bathe in this wonderful freedom, which releases you from the tethers of the flesh. Receive the blessing of fullness, abundance and completeness in the flesh, which is offered by this angel.

And the second angel stands forth in a burst of brilliant, glowing, shimmering orange to touch you and awaken your creative power, allowing you to feel a connection with the creation of all existence, which is founded upon Love and Truth and peace and unity and joy. Bathe in this joy that is yours for the taking. Become renewed by this blessing that is showered upon you. Receive this blessing of creativity.

And the third angel stands forth in a burst of brilliant, shining yellow to touch you and awaken you hidden strength, your power, your will to be all that you are. Stand forth and be strong. Choose to be all that you are, with power and strength, and all that is your birthright. You have the power to make new choices that will transform your life. You have the power of discernment to choose new patterns that will serve the Spirit. Bathe in this wonderful elixir and march forth with strength and determination. Receive this blessing of strength and courage to choose all that is offered by the third angel.

And the forth angel stands forth in a burst of gold and green with warming, soothing, calming rays. The angel touches your entire being, lifting you up, filling you with comfort, compassion, acceptance and Love, so great that all of life becomes one in Love. Feel this transforming Light touch your first, second and third chakras. Bathe in the healing power of Love. Allow every cell of your being to be touched, to glow, glisten, and be cleansed so you may fly free and be one with all of life. Receive this blessing of Love from the fourth angel.

The fifth angel stands forth in a burst of Light so blue and clear and pure that all which was unknown is now known. Truth is at your feet. All that you desire in life, past, present and future is now before you. Walk forth in strength. Choose to accept the challenges which clear the way, those challenges which thin that veil more and more, that all of life becomes one, one with you, one with all. Seek diligently in prayer for the strength and guidance and have faith that all will be well to walk forth onto eternity. Walk forth and receive the blessing of the fifth angel, which you may manifest in the flesh, Truth offered by your Spirit.

The sixth angel walks forth in a burst of Light. Bow your head in prayer, in total acceptance of the Love of all, as you become cloaked in that most glorious indigo. All of life is one. All of Truth is one. All of existence is at your feet, and you are one with all. You see and feel and know all, as your being is raised to that vibration of unconditional Love in which all Truth becomes one with your being. Become aware of the one you truly are. Become aware of the energy you are at your birth into reality. Become aware that this is the one who seeks to manifest in the flesh. This is your true purpose, and let it be your guide. Receive this blessing of awareness that is given freely by the sixth angel.

The seventh angel stands forth in a burst of white and purple and gold. Open your inner eyes to see and feel this power. Open the eyes of your Spirit and experience life in its fullest. Feel the burst of Light embrace your entire being. Experience the unconditional Love that embraces all of existence. Gather the knowingness the Light offers, that you are accepted without condition by all of existence, for it is the Truth. Likewise, within your heart choose to accept all that you are. You now resonate with the vibration of unconditional acceptance. Within your being, you feel that total peace. You feel that total acceptance. You feel the joy, which emanates from all of creation, as it was in the beginning, and is and will be. A cup filled with the eternal Light that is presented to you. Take of the cup, drink and be filled with the knowingness of the Light of life. Receive this blessing of acceptance freely given by the seventh angel.

Take time now, you who are so dearly loved by the Light of life, to find rest in this Light. Allow the nourishment to permeate your being. Receive this sustenance for your body, mind and Spirit. You, who are dearly loved, rest, allow your Spirit to rest. Rest.

[Pause]

Take a gentle breath and relax as you slowly exhale. It is time to return to the realm of your physicality. Fill your being with thankfulness for all you have received. Give thanks to the angelic host. Give thanks for the joy and Truth and peace that you have gathered. Give thanks for the Love and acceptance that you feel and for the Light for your journey onward into eternity. Bid your companions farewell with all your Love. Take a gentle breath, relax, and as you slowly exhale, embrace the consciousness of your physicality and you open your eyes.

Prayer for the Gentle Winds

So fill me so completely that I may shine
That my life would be worthy of your embrace
As the morning sun brings joy and calm
Clearing and renewing and feeling your glow in my face.

So fill me that I may walk where there is only Light
Where there is only joy
Where there is only Love
Where there is only happiness.

So teach me to see the purity of all that is Love
And when I close my eyes in meditation
I am embraced by this Love.

So walk with me that I can walk with Love
And dance with all that embraces the Light
And dance in that magnificent Light of angels.

So take my hand that as I close my eyes.
I can journey to that place
Where the morning sun is always in the sky
Where Love and Light glows as one
From within and from without
Eternally.

So as I close my eyes
Let me feel the blessing of the Light.
For you are the Light
And I am the Light
Walking as one

Amen.

Meditation

Growing Brighter

Let me seek in all I do
To find the Truth
That calls from the depths of my Spirit.

Truth that would lift me up
To see the Light
That brightens the way.

Truth that would warm my heart
As it shines from within.

Shining in the presence of the Creator of life
Growing brighter
With each step
On the journey
On that road of Truth.

Growing brighter and brighter each day
Illumined by the Light
From within.
Amen.

Regardless of where you find yourself, the path to the Light of your Spirit is always before you. It only takes your choice to embark on the journey back to that place where the Light illumines you. Remember always that you are Light. Your Spirit is Light. Let your Light shine from within to brighten your way and upon all that you touch. Regardless of where you find yourself, it only takes your courage to shine your Light and feel the warmth and glow of joy. Each day, each moment and each choice offers the opportunity for you to grow brighter and become enlightened by the Love and Truth you feel within.

Lesson 18

Self-Realization

The journey into Light takes you to a place you have always been subconsciously seeking. At any moment in time you are on that sacred journey. Although the veil of forgetfulness has kept your eyes closed and you no longer remember who you truly are, where you came from, where you are going and why you seek to follow this path, you can use the power of choice to navigate life. On the pathway onward and upward, your eyes will once again be opened.

You are on a journey and subconsciously you know the way. Truth has been seeded within your being and it has taken root to grow and blossom in magnificence.

You are at a place on this journey where you are experiencing life in its greatest form. Your choices are based on Truth. You have become a mighty warrior of Truth. Your challenges are the opportunities that open the doorway to a place which Spirit seeks. Choosing the pathway of Truth will fulfill the desires of the Spirit and manifest the eternal happiness for which you intrinsically search.

You are a mighty being of creation, a warrior of Light. You are the exemplification of Truth, manifesting here in this three-dimensional reality, firmly seeded and ready to blossom into the shining being that is your birthright. You are ready to transcend these three dimensions, walking forth onward and upward into the Light.

Walk forth on this journey of Truth, the geometry in life's architecture, which creates Light, your Light, which is the magnificent Light of your being, of your reality. This is the way and the Truth that gathers the Light, your Light, which shines here and beyond into the vastness of eternity.

This is the day, the moment you have chosen to move onward, blossoming as a magnificent being, empowered by Truth and Light, empowered by the seeds, which you call from the depths of your being. This is the moment when you seek expression, fertile soil to manifest the kingdom of Light.

Take time to embrace this Truth and become empowered and guided by Truth, along that pathway onward and upward on the journey into eternity.

This is the place and the time to connect with that divine energy, that elixir of life which manifests growth and transformation. Receive of the nourishing balm so the seeds may grow and blossom in your reality.

If you choose to make this connection, the Light of the creation will nourish you and bring growth. Truth will flow like rivers of pure water from the depths of your being. Such is the design of life. It is natural and can be viewed from the perspective of science as the geometry of life architecture. If you choose to embrace this Truth, it will bring Light to your being.

If you choose to grow in Light, you are part of that grand architecture of existence. You will transcend this reality becoming all that you are, an ambassador of Light in this corner of existence. You will become one with the Light of creation, according to the grand design of the totality of existence.

Illumination

This Is Thy Life

Speak thy Truth in the greatest form.
Speak it in all you do and say.
For this is the way.

This is the way of life.
This is the way of Love.
This is the way of all.
This is the way of one.

This do this day.
This do each day.
This is thy life.
Amen.

Truth comes to you when you least expect it. Early in the morning as the sun crosses the horizon stirring the atmosphere, creating mist and mystical apparitions among the trees and mountains, so also does Truth emerge from within. Look closely at its beauty. Wait patiently for the fog to clear. Embrace the purity of the Light.

Lesson 19

Speak out of Love

Listen to the guidance of your own Spirit as you hear these words in the silence of your heart.

"Speak words that will not control nor seek to change. Speak only that Truth which comes from within. All that is life is a manifestation of Truth and Love. Love does not control but allows one to find Truth from within."

Lesson 20

Embrace Life

Life, the question, remains. When you are lost in a place where nothing exists, how and where do you find reality? Is it beyond what the physical senses can perceive?

How do you find and know and live Truth when the perception of a greater life is hidden from your mind? You stop, look and listen and wait for inspiration. If nothing happens, what next?

How do you find Truth that transcends and takes you to a reality with many mansions in another realm? (Study the teaching of the Nazarene Master in the Book of John, chapter 14, verse 2.)

The mysteries of life prevail as nothingness beckons and opens the door. Is your house built upon a rock? Are your feet planted firmly on the ground? Do you know the fabric of life? Have you embraced it and made it your own? Are you clothed in a coat of many colourful yarns?

A mighty opportunity, your life, is unfolding before your eyes. The opportunity to transcend is before your feet. You have been called, and you have heard that voice.

What is beyond that door which is open before you? What will you do? You can fight a good fight and wield a mighty sword, the sword of Truth, as life is unfolding. Take heed. Embrace what is before you. Embrace life.

Reflection

Tomorrow

Tomorrow I will be,
But tomorrow never comes,
For tomorrow is only an illusion.

Therefore, I am,
And will be all that I am.

Now,
And in this very moment,
And with each breath.

Each moment is a treasure. Each breath is an opportunity to manifest all that you are. You are an infinite number of possibilities. Each thought offers a possibility. Each breath provides the energy to manifest that thought. Choose to live that treasure, and experience joy that cannot be described in words. Don't let the opportunities disappear, for now is the time and this is the moment. Each breath is a moment. Your consciousness holds the power to manifest the life you choose. Breathe and choose.

Lesson 21

Seek Your Truth

Sometimes you may feel that there are no simple answers to questions about life. Realize that the wisdom to guide you along the way lies within. Truth lies within. It is your Spirit which guides you to the place of wisdom and Truth.

Intrinsically, you seek wisdom and the Truth to guide you on your journey into Light. You must realize that all answers lie within. The source of all Truth is within. In your quest for Truth, you are not alone. You are a Light shining like a star in the sky, and like a glorious night, everywhere there are stars glistening and brightening existence.

Questions arise from within. The mind is always curious with desire to know what life is about, why you are here, where you have been and where you are going. You feel a desire to understand all that is life, and to know the relationship between Spirit and flesh. You have discovered that life is much greater than what the mind can fully perceive. It is this Truth you seek to embrace. It is here that you will find your Spirit, that part of your being which extends beyond your physicality to embrace totality.

How do you connect with that part of your being which lies beyond the boundaries of the mind? Truth will lead you to that door, and meditation will open it. It will take strength and courage to walk through. You already have within all that is needed to embrace the fullness of life. You need only to choose to follow that path. Follow your heart and the desires of your own Spirit and you will be guided to the Light, the star that you are.

What will you find? You will see the Truth: You are a magnificent creation of Light. Is it a mighty grid work of Light fashioned out of the glory of all Truth, which extends to the farthest reaches of eternity? You are that magnificent creation. You are a creator of this Light, which embraces ALL of existence as one.

Your journey takes you along a pathway paved with Truth. Truth is realized out of choices when you face life's challenges. Choose to embrace Truth with the understanding that it is and has always been your birthright and an intrinsic part of your being. Embrace your essence, which is Truth. As you grow and expand to embrace your totality, you will awaken the memory of all your sojourns, thereby opening the door to transformation. Your choices will open the door to Light, which will integrate into your reality.

Therefore, take time to seek Truth. Take time to understand the way of Truth and the path it offers. Truth may come to you through your dreams. It may come to you as you write in your journal. Truth may come when you interact with your neighbour, or at the most unexpected time and place. Be prepared. Be expectant.

If you choose to follow the path of spiritual growth, you must consecrate your entire being so you may become the worthy channels of Truth in all your sleeping and waking hours.

Seek your Truth, embrace Truth and become one with life which is all that you are, as you journey onward and upward into Light. Amen.

Reflection

Choose Thou

When you express Truth
Explore the energy that stirs within.

This is the source of life
Your life force.

To express Truth is a choice.

It is choice that opens the door of life.
It is choice that carves a new reality.
One paved with Truth
One that blossoms with Love.

Choose thou.

Reflection

The Commitment

It is a whole life commitment.
It goes beyond the classroom.
It goes beyond Sunday worship.
It goes beyond the daily meditation.
It goes beyond the annual fasting.
It goes beyond constant prayers.

It is in all of these and more.
It is the dedication of your whole life.

Each moment and each breath,
Directed towards the manifestation of the Spirit,
in the oneness with the flesh.

Realize that life emerges from within, and it is choice that navigates your path to that place which is the source of your life. It is the source of Truth, Love and joy. All of these are basic ingredients of life. It is who you are. You are already there. Take and drink and live. Your purpose here is to live; therefore, live life to the fullest. Choose wisely as you navigate your pathway. The choices may be simple and trivial, but each choice impacts your whole life. Each tiny choice becomes part of who you are. Thus, as you choose in each moment and each breath, let the source be from within, the place of Love and Truth, knowing that such integrity only offers joy that is eternal. Thus, forget not who you are and your purpose. Live and be merry, for it is your purpose, and guided by Love and Truth, the source, which lies within, will fulfill the desires of your Spirit. Be committed to yourself and you will reap the rewards of eternal happiness. You are the beneficiary of your choices in each moment and with each breath.

Illumination

Faith

Know you not what you live by
For the voice calls from within and beckons you on
And the Truth of life speaks to you.
Truth calls your name.

There is no life without faith.
For in faith you have your being.
Faith is the vessel which holds the Spirit.
Faith is the bridge between the flesh and the Spirit.

What say you that you seek?
You seek the energy of life.
You seek to know the way.
You seek the Truth.

Open your heart, dear one, and look therein
And you shall find all that you seek.
You shall find life.
You shall find all that is.

Go now and walk across that bridge.
Hold fast to the Truth that you have within.
And you shall find the way to your Spirit.
You shall find the way to the Light.

Prayer

Prayer of Thanks

I shall fill my heart with thankfulness
For Love
For Light
For Truth
For the understanding of my fears.

I will fill my heart with the desire for guidance
That my fears may be dissolved with Love
That I may be free
To fly beyond
To that glorious place
I can call home.
Amen.

Prayer

Prayer of Protection

I give thanks for the presence of the Creator in my life and ask for guidance as I embark on this journey onward. I seek the protection of the angels, to surround and guard me as I walk through the valley of the shadows, seeking Truth and Love, the essence of life, on my journey upward into Light. Amen.

Lesson 24

Live and Let Live

The time has come to look to the sky and find a place that is blue and focus there.

The wind will come and fill the sky with clouds and the blue will soon disappear.

It is Truth that will guide you to the place of blue, which lies beyond the clouds. It is a place that will remain blue throughout eternity.

It is Truth that will open your eyes so you can see as Spirit, beyond the clouds.

It is Truth that will open the door, revealing the pathway that transcends this realm.

Within are the seeds of emancipation, awaiting your call to awaken and take root. As the sun rises, the Light clears the clouds, bringing nourishing rain and revealing once again that place of blue.

The vision of life beyond this realm is being realized in your heart. Live Truth, for Truth lives within and shall always be so.

Prayer

Prayer of Hope

I give thanks for the Light that shines upon my path, showing me the way to a reality beyond the clouds.

I give thanks for the Truth that opens the door to the Light.

I give thanks for the opportunity to embrace this Truth.

I give thanks for strength to embrace Truth and become one with Truth.

I give thanks for this faith and hope in Truth and life.

I give thanks for the strength to grow with hope.

I give thanks for wisdom to choose the way of Truth that transcends this realm, embracing a new reality, a new earth, the pathway home. Amen.

Lesson 25

The Breath

Breathe in, hold, feel the beat of your heart as life-giving energy flows, touching every cell of your body. Close your eyes and embrace the oneness of life as you exhale.

Lesson 26

The Blessings of a Child

It is truly a wonderful blessing when a child speaks to you, for there is no judgment. Receive this blessing of the pure at heart.

Observe the children. They Love without condition or expectation. They judge not, exercising only the purity of unconditional acceptance. They seek joy. They manifest their desires.

Life is about laughing and playing as you see in the heart of a child.

Within, you are a child, but you have judged yourself as being an adult. It is time to transcend this judgment, freeing the child within, to laugh and play and dance once more.

Illumination

Affirmations of the Spirit

To be all that I am
I will uncover myself and become a Light
Shining in the darkness.

I am and will be free.
I am and will be in command of my being.
I am and will be a living example.
I am and will be free to walk as Spirit.
I am and will be in command of the flesh.
I am and will be the manifestation of Love.
I am and will be the manifestation of Truth.
I am and will be all that I am.

Lesson 27

Affirmations

Affirmations hold a sacred vibration. They resonate. You resonate. You can resonate with a vibration that you choose. Embrace a vibration of your choice in your going and coming. Each day, each moment, each challenge can be faced with a chosen vibration.

Therefore, choose. Unite with the vibration that you have chosen. Let all your interactions be transformed by the vibration that you choose in each day, each hour and each moment.

Choose a unique affirmation for each day. Have one for each hour, and one for each moment. Choose and thereby command your life to be all that you are.

Meditation

The Notes

I AM.
I see.
I speak.
I live.
I will.
I feel.
I Love.

(Inspired by the Edgar Cayce readings)

Meditation

The Music

I am all that I am.
I see with eyes of my Spirit.
I speak with the voice of Truth.
I live in abundance.
I will overcome the flesh.
I feel new life.
I Love without condition.

Reflection

Manifest Your Desire

"I AM THAT I AM."
"I AM" and will manifest all "THAT I AM."
"I AM" a Light shining with Love and Truth.
My power is the Light that "I AM."

I will show Love and acceptance to all.
I will choose to manifest my power in each moment.

As you experience life and face challenges, list the affirmations that will help increase your vibration in each moment, to help steer you along the pathway of the life that you choose.

Your desire is the power of your Spirit. As you choose your affirmations, let them manifest the desire of the Spirit, in your going out and coming in.

Reflection

When You Speak

When you speak, understand the ones before you. Understand the flow of energy. It is the inquiring minds that seek to shine. Like baby chicks, it is ego (hunger) that is reaching to be the first to get the worm (Love) and satisfy a longing within. It is incumbent upon you to foster a receptive state of calm.

Seek, therefore, the path of Truth. Follow the connection that each hold with Truth. You will touch their Spirits, bringing peace and calm, for it is a connection with Spirit that each truly seek. Fulfill this desire and you will plant seeds of Love.

Open your heart and listen to their yearning, for in their emptiness they reach out to you.

With the Love that flows from your Spirit, heed this call, soothe their tired Spirits and feed their emptiness. Open a channel through which Truth flows freely, satisfying the longing of their Spirits, and thereby forges bonds of Love.

Reflection

The Cloak of Truth

Why do you clothe your body?
Is it simply for protection from the elements?
Is it the persona you project?
Is it to hide who you are?

Do you hide the Truth?
Do you hide your Spirit?
Do you hide your Love?
Do you hide all that you are?

What is your Truth?
Do you shine the Light from your heart?
Are you illuminated by the Truth you hold within?

Expose yourself.
Expose your Truth.
Expose your true self.
Shine the Light from your heart.
Shine the Light of the Spirit within.
It is who you are.
It is all that you are.
Amen.

Illumination

Honour Yourself

It is your life.

Honour your Truth.
Honour your feelings.
Honour your desires.

You have hopes.
You have dreams.

Honour your freewill to choose,
To create, to be all that you are.

Honour all that emanates from within,
For you are a Light shining from the centre of your being
With desires, hopes, feelings and dreams.

Add colour to your being.
Your choice is the salt.
You are the flame.

Honour yourself.
Shine.
Sparkle.

Meditation

The Word

The word is power.
The crucible of the Spirit
A force manifest.

The word became the Light.
I am a spark of Light.
I am the word.

I am the living word.
The word manifest
The word made flesh.

The word is life.
The word is the Spirit.
I am the Spirit manifest as flesh.

I am the power, the Light, and the word.
I am the crucible of the Spirit.
I am the word made into flesh.
I am the word.

Illumination

I Am the Living Word

When I speak
It is my word that is a reflection of the Spirit.
My Spirit is my word.
And my word is my Spirit.

When I speak
It is Truth that is carried upon breath.
It is Truth that flows from within.
Truth is my life.

When I speak
It is Love that flows from my heart.
Love is the lifeblood of my Spirit.
My Spirit is Love.

When I speak
It is my word that I speak.
My word is my life.
And my life is the living word.

Meditation

I Speak

I speak the words of the "I AM."
I speak the words of the Spirit.
I speak the words of Truth.

I speak with words that fulfill my physical life.
I speak with words that guide my path.
I speak with words that create life.

I speak with words of Love.
Amen.

Chapter Four

The Bread of Life

Introduction

Take time to meditate and sparkle with brilliance. Take time each day to unite with the Light of your Spirit.

At the dawn of life, there was Light. Life in this realm is a manifestation of that Light. Choose to shine with purity and brilliance as it was in the beginning. The Spirit is Light. As it is in Spirit, so let it be in the flesh. Choose to shine the Light of the Spirit through the flesh. Choose to grow with this Light. It is your birthright.

You can perceive the physical realm as a place of learning and healing. As the Light of the Spirit shines upon this realm through your physicality, likened to the scientific principles of a rainbow, colours become visible. In this realm, you are a rainbow of Light. All of life is energy. You are energy. Energy radiates colour. Each component of your being shines with a different colour, which is your aura. When all the colours shine with purity and unite as one, you glow with a white light.

As you think and feel, your energy changes, and this is visible in your aura. Here, in this school and this hospital, you have the opportunity to address all the parts of your being, to grow, change, heal and shine with the totality of your brilliance and be filled with a joy that is eternal. It is truly a journey into Light. As you embark upon this journey, realize that you are in a realm of abundance. Take, eat and live in the glory of the Light.

Feel That Red Glow

Balance is created and maintained by choice. Your existence here in this realm is a function of balance between flesh and Spirit. Spirit reaches out into the physical realm by means of the flesh. To function fully, balance must be maintained. Perfect physical health is a natural result of balance, required to effectively manifest the desires of Spirit.

Your energy centres or chakras are like the finger of Spirit reaching out to play a musical instrument, your physical body. The music is your life. Chakras influence the endocrine system, which governs your physicality. Go into meditation and embrace the consciousness of Spirit, and you will see this as you look through the eyes of Spirit. You will see the flow of energy and shades of colour emanating from the energy of life. The endocrine system in turn is linked to organs. The health of your organs governs their ability to manifest the instructions from the endocrine system. The health of your organs not only determines the health of your entire physical body, but also the ability to manifest the desires of Spirit.

Choose total health as your way of being. Nourish the body. Do not be deceived by an environment which seeks to manipulate the perception of health and beauty for material gain. Why be concerned about the outer appearance? Choose to become cognizant of that part of your being responsible for feelings, thoughts, attitudes, emotions and intentions, all of which emanate from within, a fire that will either temper or destroy. Let the Spirit that offers Truth and Love be your guide.

The earth, air, water and sun sustain the body. These are the basic elements of life. It is the same for all physical life in this realm. Choose all that is pure and sufficient to maintain balance.

The Earth provides food and shelter. Whatever you require for survival, it is here and she gives of herself freely and lovingly. Realize that any restriction or lack of abundance that is perceived has been created of your own accord and is a function of the physical mind. The Earth is kind and patient, bearing all your demands, excess and abuse. She smiles each day at dawn as you are bathed with golden Light. She shares so much to satisfy all your physical desires.

If you accept and live this Truth, your aura will shine with a pure, brilliant, red Light flowing from the centre of your being and harmonizing with the Light the Earth radiates. The Earth recognizes this oneness as an expression of your Love and acceptance.

As you walk this path, shining, resonating with the vibration of red, you not only harmonize with the Earth, but also with everyone and everything that emits this energy. It is a synergistic path of acceptance, enrichment, abundance, contentment and growth.

Accept the lessons of the birds that neither sow nor toil, yet need nothing. They are adorned with wonderful colours, sing melodious tunes and are fed from the harvest of nature's vast gardens. As the Nazarene Master shared, you are far more than the birds and flowers. Accept these lessons with faith, strength and courage, and manifest your brilliance by gracing your aura with a luminous red glow.

Your journey onward and upward embraced by this Light will take you to a place of transcendence where sustenance is in abundance and of a higher source.

First Chakra Meditation

The purpose of this meditation is to harmonize body, mind and Spirit to expand the energy from the area of the first chakra. The first chakra corresponds with the sexual glands (ovaries and testes). The symbol to hold in your mind in this meditation is the "bread" of life. Focus on sustenance that is both spiritual and physical. The aura this energy radiates is a brilliant red.

At this stage of meditation, attention is focused in the lower part of the body, in the area between the anus and sexual glands. Keep in mind that the reproductive glands correspond with the first chakra, and it is your connection with the earth, growth and creativity. This is the area where Spirit and cells unite to manifest life. It is the area that is responsible for health and physical growth. It is the area where you hold your power to manifest life.

In a state of balance, the energy of life flows from above. The guidance that you seek shines like a brilliant white Light from the seventh chakra. It expands to the fourth and then to the first chakra, filling your entire being with Light and touching all the chakras. The energy of Love from the fourth chakra expands and spills over onto the lower chakras to temper attitudes. It is the energy in the first chakra that enables Spirit and cells to unite in the process of creation. It is the attitudes, which you hold within, that determine the nature of life that you create.

Flesh or Spirit, what will you feed? Will you accept the guidance offered by Spirit or will you allow the flesh to have control? You have free will to embrace the power of choice. It is your free will to transcend old patterns and embrace new ones. It is your free will to accept the guidance flowing from the seventh chakra, and choose Love to deliver this guidance, unfettering Spirit from the controls of the flesh by tempering the activities of the first chakra. Such is the way of balance in which you shine from the crown all the way to the base, filling your aura with a brilliant red glow.

Prayer
Before you go into meditation, take the time to pray. As you pray, become aware of your physical, mental and spiritual aspirations. Within this awareness, realize that the benefits of meditation are gained when you find internal harmony, when body, mind and Spirit function as one in state of balance. Balance is achieved by maintaining a clear conscience in all your actions and thoughts. When there is balance, the mind remains calm and unobtrusive. It is a whole life activity. If your whole life is balanced, the door to the meditative state will swing open easily, and a still mind will allow your Spirit to emerge and touch your consciousness.

Fear not, for life is a journey of awakening which leads to the Light, one step at a time. You have taken steps, which have brought you to this place. Give thanks for the guidance, which brought you here to a place of seeking. Reach out to your higher self to guide you in your meditations and as you journey onward. Seek guidance from all the energies, which offer the blessings of Light, Love and Truth for your journey. Seek the protection offered by the Light of Creation to surround you with Love and Truth, as you enter the gates of meditation.

Physical Preparation
Meditation is a whole life activity. Although you have chosen this time, this moment, to go into the silence, remember that your physical state is determined not only by choices in the moment, but also by those made in the past. Become cognizant of this in your daily activities and make choices that navigate your whole life on a path devoted to the aspirations of the Spirit. Remember that the body is a temple housing this Spirit. As you prepare for meditation, you are preparing the body as a living sacrifice unto your Spirit.

Spirit functions optimally when there is total health. Become aware of your diet, your attire, the air that you breathe and the water you drink. Become aware of the Light that shines upon you, and the sounds that press upon your ears. Become aware of what is before your eyes and the surroundings that reflect their light upon your eyes. They all play a part in the function of the body as a vessel of the Spirit.

Choose a time to meditate. Be regular and punctual. It is the choices you make in the moment and throughout your life which open the gateways of the flesh for the manifestation of the Spirit. Fear not, for you have chosen to be here at this moment, on this pathway.

Choose a place where you will not be disturbed. Choose an environment that offers the gentle stimulation of peace and quiet that will cradle your entire being. Realize that you are choosing an ashram or a sanctuary. Before you enter, be cleansed both in body and mind. Wear sufficiently comfortable clothing. Approach with honour and respect as you prepare to embrace the silence of the Light.

To free Spirit from the encumbrances of the flesh, head, neck, shoulder and spinal chord exercises offer a source of relaxation, relieving accumulated tension and blockages. Sit comfortably on a chair where your feet can be flat on the floor and very slowly and gently extend your head, forward, backward, sideways and in a circular motion, activating your entire spine. The key here is gently and slowly. Each of the six steps in this exercise will require two to three minutes. With this motion, feel each muscle and vertebra as they adjust to release tension. As you release the tension from your neck and shoulders, you will feel the desire to extend this movement down the spine and eventually all the way to the tip of the toes, flexing, releasing and revitalizing every muscle, joint and cell. As this happens, realize that Spirit is now guiding you. Embrace this guidance. It is a path upon which all the tension is released, opening a doorway to freedom from mind and body. It is a state in which Spirit can fly free to embrace all that is Love and Truth, unencumbered by the flesh.

Posture

Use a pleasing position, one that can be maintained for the period of time you choose to meditate. It is important to sit in a comfortable position, with your spine gently erect. This will help the flow of energy through the spiritual centres of the body. You can choose to sit on a chair with your feet gently placed flat on the floor, thighs flat on the chair and palms on your thighs. If you can, face the sun when you meditate, east in the morning and west in the evening. Always allow your Spirit to be your guide as you choose.

Grounding

Grounding is paramount whenever you meditate. It is a state in which you are in command of your being. It is a state in which you are surrounded by the Light of Love and Truth.

There are energies or entities hovering in the realms around you, seeking to manifest their will and desires through your physicality. They can use devious means to trick you into thinking that it is your own desire. Thus, always be alert. This can only happen with your choice. Surround yourself with the Light of Love and Truth offered from the realms above, from within and from the earth below.

Make that physical connection between the energies from the realm above, through your physicality to the earth beneath you. Feel the golden energy pouring down upon you, passing through the crown, filling your entire being and uniting with the energy of the earth below. You are the connecting point. As you prepare to meditate, become energized like a light bulb with the power that passes through you, as you feel connected with the all-embracing energy of life.

Know who you are. Know from where you came. Know where you are going. Know your purpose. Know your Truth. Know the power of Love. Know your aspirations. Feel all these as part of your being. Become one with the totality of life. Know that this is your birthright and your true nature. It is all that is natural. You are embracing your true self.

Breathing

Go directly to the source of all Light and seek permission to approach. Seek permission to breathe in the Light, this elixir, this healing balm that connects all. Breathe, and allow the Light to touch your Spirit.

As you breathe, allow the Light to bathe your entire body with a purifying and cleansing energy. Allow the Light to activate each cell with life-giving force, making each cell glow. Allow the Light to transform each cell into pure energy. Feel the transforming Light shine from the Creator of Life, pour onto your crown, permeate your very being, penetrating, filtering between the cells and filling you with peace and Love.

With each gentle and continuous breath, take the time to go within and find that place where you feel most connected with the Creator of Life.

With each breath, transform [fourth chakra] your passion [second chakra] into pure Love [fourth chakra]. Enter the glory of the Truth [sixth chakra] that you hold within.

As you breathe, remember that you are Spirit, housed in a body of flesh, a temple [first chakra], with a mind that can be used as a tool for transformation [seventh chakra].

As you breathe, you can transcend the perceptions of the physical that are so well-defined by the mind [third chakra].

You can move to that higher realm of consciousness [sixth chakra] that is guided by the Spirit [seventh chakra]. You can move to that realm of Truth [fifth chakra] where you are embraced by the purity of Love [fourth chakra].

As you breathe, become one with this Love and Truth. Become one with your Spirit. Become one with the infinite.

As you breathe, find that place within, where you can meet with the Creator of Life. Seek the blessings of the Creator of Life as you approach.

Feel the peace and Love as you inhale and hold this energy within your being. As you breathe, allow the energy to do its work within you, transforming each cell of your being to its purest crystalline form. With the gentle rhythm of your breath, move closer and closer to that transforming white Light of the Creator of Life. Become one with the Light.

Balancing the Chakras
When you are ready, inhale gently and allow a burst of the whitest and purest Light to flow through your crown. Feel the Light shine upon you as it enters your crown, making its way to the base chakra and back up, filling your entire being with Light.

On the way down, the white Light moves to the sixth chakra, also known as the third eye, the area of insight. It is the area where your Spirit emerges to embrace your physicality.

Spirit is willing. Is the flesh willing? Is the mind willing? As you breathe, you can choose to allow the white Light to activate this chakra, fulfilling the purpose of Spirit, emerging to unite as one with the flesh. It is the emerging of the "I AM" consciousness.

If you so choose, seek balance in your life. Address the events of the past, releasing that which no longer serves you, thereby opening the door so Spirit may enter, planting seeds for a new tomorrow.

Receive of this Light and shine from your very core, from each chakra, from each cell, that you may see and feel all the colours of the rainbow, which you are. Rejoice in what you see. Feel the vibration of the indigo Light which surrounds you. See and feel and become one with Love and Truth that flows from within, and all that surrounds you in Love and Truth, as Spirit unites as one with the flesh. Rejoice in the Light.

The white Light travels to the fifth chakra bringing balance, thereby strengthening your will and weaving a foundation of power to transcend the flesh, manifesting your Truth. Allow your Light to shine with a brilliant blue aura. Feel the power of the sword of Truth within you. Feel the grips of your hand ready and willing to embrace this power and manifest your Truth.

The white Light travels to the base. Allow it to activate the base chakra, the sacred place of solace where cells and Spirit unite.

Feel the base chakra become a pure and a brilliant red. The chakra rotates. Feel the colour and hear the sweet sound of the vibration as it resonates through your entire body. See the glow of pure red as it emanates to surround you and fill your aura.

The white Light now travels up the spine to the third chakra, the area of the mind which holds patterns from your lifetimes. It is the doorway of transformation. Feel the transforming energy of the white Light as a channel to guidance and Love, balancing the third chakra. Feel the vibration within as your aura as it glows with brilliant yellow.

See the white Light travel to the second chakra bringing balance. Focus on this place of creativity. Allow the white Light to energize and transform. Feel the brilliant orange energy, and listen to the sound as the emanation fills your aura.

The white Light travels to the area of the heart. Feel the Love from the fourth chakra unite with the white Light as it moves up and down your spine. Feel the transforming power of Love fill your first, second and third chakra, transforming and bringing balance. Feel the power of this transforming energy of Love as it delivers you from the pangs of the flesh. Allow the Light which resonates from your heart centre to embrace your entire being and temper all your thoughts and actions with Love. Feel the pure, brilliant green Light as it bursts forth, filling your aura.

See the white Light travel to the crown and encircle your entire head with a brilliant glow, spilling over to embrace the entire body. Feel the warmth of violet with a core of white as it permeates your being and resonates with the power of the "I AM" presence. You are the "I AM." Allow this power to expand and fill your entire aura, touching all who choose to feel the Love and Truth of the Creator of life.

Now that the seven chakras have been energized, you may remain in this state of silence for a time of your choosing, as you continue with your meditation.

When there is balance, there is Light. When there is Light, there is balance. As your body, mind and Spirit become so attuned, it takes only a single moment to embrace the fullness of the Light. Be patient, for progress comes slowly. Your journey here took an eternity. The return will only take a moment. Prepare with patience for this moment.

It is time to focus once more on the first chakra, the area that is bursting with a pure, brilliant red energy.

Flower of the Lotus

See yourself as a lotus, gently floating upon a pond of clear, pure water, crowned in the silence of a starlit night. In the distant horizon, the haze of a purple and pink sky signals that it is dawn.

The birds sing to the melody of a new day as the darkness slowly disappears to reveal the Light of a crimson sky.

Breathe in the energy that fills the sphere.

The entire landscape is bathed with crimson as the Light filters through the trees. The birds dance about in merriment. You can feel the energy of the spheres touch everything and surround you. Breathe in this energy, allowing it to fill your entire being.

The day grows brighter as the colours in the sky change to crimson and gold. A gentle breeze welcomes the warmth of the morning sun as she peeps over the horizon. In silence, you feel the touch of her energy. As you breathe, allow this energy to fill your heart and flow to the base chakra.

The waters glisten and sparkle with gold as the rays of Light filter through the leaves. With the gentle touch of the Light, the flower shines with joy, ready to explode in colour.

As you meditate, feel that flower within your heart, ready to burst in its splendour, sharing its beauty with the Love it radiates. Reach out to touch every cell of your being and shine, for you are a being who is Love. Your brilliance brings Light to the life that abounds.

Wake up to the voice of the Light that calls to your heart to exude, from its very core, the radiance of Love.

Breathe slowly and gently as you see and feel this within.

Like a tree of Light feel your Love grow, flowing from your

heart-source like blood to nourish your being, filling your base chakra.

Feel your base chakra become energized, the bread of life that feeds your entire being with life-giving nourishment, where Spirit and cells unite to create life, your life, embraced by the Love which flows from your heart, embraced by the Love that flows from the Creator of life. As you meditate, become so energized that your life will feed only upon this source of nourishment in all that she creates, and the fruits that you bear are from her seeds of Love.

You are Light. You are the source, the energy of life. Fill existence with all that you are. You are a flower of Love, growing, shining, blossoming, nourished by the Light. Become all that you are, a flower of Light.

Closing

As a flower of Light, it is time to return from where you came. Give thanks for all you have received. Embrace and assimilate. Realize that you are Spirit, housed in the flesh, and it is time to return to the physical, embraced by the Light that filled your being. Take time now to gently reawaken and embrace the consciousness of your physicality. As you become aware of your physical surroundings, you may gently open your eyes. Amen.

Prayer of Thanks

I give thanks for this time of meditation, to embrace the Light and be filled with peace, Love and Truth. I give thanks for the opportunity to grow and transform, and to once again walk in this realm, embraced by the Light.

I give thanks for the embrace of the healing Light. I pray that this blessing remains with me as I journey onward through life.

I give thanks to all my guides and teachers, and all who inspire me to embrace Love and Truth. I give thanks to the angels. I give thanks to the legions who walked behind me to protect me, beside me to counsel me and before me to guide me.

I seek the blessing of such protection, guidance and council as I journey onward and upward into Light. Amen.

Reflection

Dawn

It is early in the morning.
The sky blinks and wipes her eyes.
Then she smiles,
Her smile so radiant.
The world awakens to behold her beauty.

Her gentle eyes blink slowly
As she looks down upon me
In silent pleasure.
Her freckled face glows.
Like an angel, her hair lights up.

And my mind wanders away to the distant horizon.
To embrace such beauty,
That only God can create.
Sunrise!

The process of enlightenment can be likened to the sunrise as you become illuminated by the Light of your Spirit shining from within.

Lesson 28

Being

In each moment
With each feeling
Against each challenge
From each chakra
By each word
Upon each prayer
Be one with Spirit.

Lesson 29

Meditation

In the heaven of my consciousness
Is the one that I am.

My Truth.
My word.

And it is with my will
That I manifest here on Earth
All that I am.

Creating
Transforming
With Love.

Being all that I am
Here in the flesh
As it is in the heavenly consciousness
Of the one that I truly am.

Lesson 30

Yet It Is Your House

Your house!
The place you live!
The place of Love?
The place of joy?

What is the state of repair?
Is the foundation sure?
Have the walls withstood the trials of time?
Is it furnished with peace and tranquility?
Is it furnished with happiness?

Is your house built with your choice?
It is your choice that will renew.
It is your choice that will transform.
It is your choice that will restore.

What will your choice manifest?
A place of peace and tranquility?
A place of happiness?
A house built upon the rock of Truth?
A house furnished with Love?
A house that is filled with joy?

Choose.
For it is your house.

Meditation

Finding Your Centre

As you pray, take the time to breathe.

As you exhale,
Focus on the centre of your being,
Your Spirit.
Become aware of your state of being.

Are you in command?
Are your choices emerging from within?
Are you honouring yourself?
Are you commanding the mind?
Are you choosing the way of happiness?
Are you manifesting your desires?
Are you shining your light?
Are you sharing the words of your Spirit?
Are you manifesting the Love from within?
Are you manifesting the Truth from within?
Are you being all that you are?

Let your prayers and meditations bring you back to your centre, your Spirit, where you are in command, responding to life with the courage to choose what you know is the Truth.

Lesson 31

Is There a Plan?

Life brings many challenges. As you walk through the door each morning, you are not even aware of what may befall you. You walk with a certain faith as you enter the world of the unknown without giving any thought regarding life, such as what you are doing here and where you are going. Even though you know who you are and that you are being guided, and you know that the Creator of life is with you, it is your free will that allows you to travel the sinuous path of life, without care or concern.

In moments of quiet reflection, you ask yourself: Is this the right way or is there something better? As the answers come, you make plans to change and follow a new path. Then the next day comes and you walk out the door without giving a second thought about your life, where you are going and the challenges that may greet you along the way. So the cycle of your life continues. On and on you merrily go and where you stop no one knows.

Many live this way without realizing that life can change by the end of that very day, in an instant. Think for a moment what could happen. It is no wonder that some encounter challenges you pray will never come your way. These are the challenges that carve a path into the unknown. These are the challenges that offer difficult choices. These are the challenges that test and temper the Spirit. How do you embrace the power to direct your life? Would you have the courage to manifest your choice in the face of a difficult challenge, if it appears in the next instant?

When faced with a challenge, do you feel that you have the freedom to choose? Do you know what you would like to choose for your tomorrows? Have you determined your hopes and aspirations? Where would you go to find answers? Who do you ask?

When will the great teacher appear to show you the way? Where is the door to that sacred path?

Realize that the answer lies within. All answers lie within. The answers are in manifesting the Truth you find within, no matter what they are. It is a door that is before you, ready for you to reach out, take the latch and open. It is within your power, available for you to choose, and there for you to manifest.

What are the desires of your Spirit? Ponder the changes you envision in your life to live the way you feel you should, materially and spiritually. This is the place to start. It is the first stone in the house that you are about to build, and your Spirit holds the blueprint.

As you meditate, look within and determine what is needed to lay the next stone in your house, then another, and so on. Build a foundation strong and sure, unshakable by the winds of change that may unexpectedly blow your way.

Take time to seek inspiration from the Creator of life, the angels, and all those who are about you, reaching out to you with Love and Truth. Choose to formulate a plan for your life and work with it. Choose a path based upon Love and Truth as desired by the Spirit. Choose to build a mansion with a foundation of Truth, shaped by Love and filled with joy, one small step at a time.

Prayer

Prayer of Invocation

Dear Creator of life
I pray that you be with me
(Take a deep breath)
To fill my heart and body
And my entire being
With your presence
(Take a deep breath).

I pray that you surround me
With your white Light of protection
(Take a deep breath)
And fill me with your glowing presence
(Take a deep breath)
To guide, comfort and lead me
(Take a deep breath).

I pray that you walk with me now
(Take a deep breath).
I invite the angels,
I invite the masters,
I invite my guides and teachers
To inspire me
To teach me
To show me that door to the Light in my heart
(Take a deep breath).
Amen.

Reflection

Change

Nothing remains the same.
Everything changes.

Through experience
You learn.
You grow.

You change.
You move on.

Such is the way of life.
Such is the way of all life.
Amen.

On your journey, you are faced with many challenges. Change is natural and necessary for growth. The growth you seek is the embrace of Light, or enlightenment. When the Light of the Spirit shines through the flesh, this is enlightenment. Thus, accept the challenges that befall you and face them with courage and strength, choosing to manifest the Light of your Spirit, paving a new path that will change your life.

Meditation

Will You but Knock

What is my purpose?
What are my aspirations?
What do I seek to manifest?
What is the intention of my being?
What do I hold in my imagination?
What is the blueprint of my tomorrow?
What thoughts do I send into the ethers?

I am but a cup, empty and I thirst.

I call upon my Spirit
To fill me.

Meditation

The Answer

It is Love
It is Truth
To be.

You will know
When you are there
That this is the answer.

As you take time to meditate, let it not be a time for the musing of the mind, nor a time to rest the body, for you are here to seek oneness with the Spirit. Although it may appear difficult, and you may feel that you are simply human, and perhaps only the gurus (teachers) from far countries on mountaintops can truly meditate, you are no less than anyone. You were born with the moon and stars, just like the gurus. It is true that your journeys were perhaps different and you are at different places on your journey, but your goals are one and the same. The place you seek to be is the same. You are flesh and blood, which clothe the Spirit, and it is this Spirit you seek to embrace and within whose arms you will find the comfort that you seek. It is the same for all. You are not different. Yet, you are unique. Much like each star in the sky is unique, each shining with individual beauty, your smile and Light is as unique as the stars. Therefore, when you meditate, seek to shine. Seek to find that place of oneness. Seek to resonate with the Light of your Spirit which is Truth and Love, and when you are there, you will know. With practice, you will know how to get there easily. With practice, you will feel the Love and Truth that you are. With practice, you will learn to shine the Light of your Spirit through the flesh.

Lesson 32

The Power of a Journal

Today is the beginning of the rest of your life. If you take the time to look within, you will see that life offers so much as you travel along its sinuous and mysterious pathways. You encounter challenges, which are the opportunities that offer renewal, so you may shine from the depths of your being and be who you truly are.

You were created as a being of Light and here in this physical realm you can shine the Light you hold within upon all that you touch. In so doing, you are manifesting the way of Spirit and your birthright. It is the desire of Spirit that you shine as a being of Light. It is your purpose for being here.

The Spirit within seeks to be all that it is. In so doing, your Spirit takes you along a path where you may once again remember your birth into Light. The desire of Spirit is to unite as one with the flesh and shine with its brilliance. As you journey through time in this physical reality, your Spirit offers such opportunities.

Each day you face numerous challenges. These challenges are the opportunities to open doors. Each doorway takes you one step closer to your place of birth.

The journey to this place of Light, where you call home, is a simple one. The Truth of the Spirit becomes the Light that will guide you along this path.

And as you walk this road, you may find many treasures, pearls of wisdom and a crown of Light. You may find the jewelled sword of Truth to fight your battles. Each victory takes you one step closer. Each victory offers Light. Each victory offers oneness with the Spirit.

Stop and listen. You will hear the gentle call. It is the voice of Truth that calls from the depths of your being, from the heart of your Spirit. Will you stop? Will you listen? Will you heed the small voice? It is always there and it is your choice. It is your free will. It is for you to command your life.

There is much work to be done. The work before you may be accomplished in different ways. Truth comes and speaks to you and gently nudges you along the pathway of Light. How do you become a noble warrior of Truth? How do you receive the pearls of wisdom? How do you gain the crown of Light? Where do you find the jewelled sword?

You have this opportunity. It is before you each day and each moment. If you will, choose to walk this path by adjusting your life to become a warrior of Light. In so doing you prepare physically and mentally to walk as Spirit in this physical realm.

How do you prepare for this task, for this journey, for this quest as a warrior of Light? How do you open the door to your Spirit, allowing Truth to flow into your conscious mind?

Truth comes in many ways. As a first step, you can explore the processes and benefits of using a journal. There is much power in this tool. You can embrace Spirit and transcribe Truth that flows from the heart of your being. Spirit will use this channel to share Truth that offers Love and guidance.

When you choose to embrace the power of using a journal, you must be committed to the process. Like the rising and setting of the sun, each day follow the patterns offered by the universe. You are physically, mentally and spiritually a component of all that exists; therefore, you can choose to do likewise. If you consider the process of nourishing and energizing your being, you will realize there is a pattern and an inner clock. Similarly, you breathe every day, each moment, bringing strength and power to your life. Yoga teaches ways to harness the power of the breath. Thus, as you harness the power of Truth and manifest it in your daily activities, it becomes firmly planted within your being, forming a firm foundation, which becomes a path to the very essence of your life. When the air or food is fresh and pure, you feel strengthened and invigorated. Expose yourself to the wisdom that is transcribed in your journal, and the possibilities in life become endless opportunities. Remember, regularity is key, so set time aside each day to stop, relax, contemplate and write the words you feel deep within the heart which in Truth is of your Spirit.

During the process of journaling, choose to be positive and creative. Receive words which offer life and Love, those that bring Light, Truth and strength. Allow only these to pass through your consciousness. Let the others go with the wind and be taken to the farthest reaches of the horizon, to rest there for eternity. Remember this statement and make it your own: My house will be one of Truth and Love and peace and caring and creativity, and therein shall dwell all that was created that is the Light of life.

When you write in your book, do so by choice only. Do so with an open heart filled with the Creator's Love, Love of self, Love of Truth and Love of life. You may choose to meditate to attune to the Light, before transcribing. In so doing, your journal becomes a tool of the Spirit within.

Journaling will take you on a journey of self-realization. You will learn of Love and acceptance. As you learn to Love self completely, more and more each day you will reveal truths that will open the door to the Creator's Light. It is the cycle of growth and transformation.

Find the courage to seek within and make choices so your house will be filled only with Light. Seek the path that brings peace and harmony to all of life. Choose wisely.

So then, what will you write? As seekers of Light and Truth, there is much that you would like to accomplish. As you sit before your journal, seek Light and Truth that help you solidify your work in this realm and beyond. Thus, each day as you make choices, as you face challenges, as you make affirmations, let this process of putting pen to paper be one of growth. At first, you may find the process somewhat challenging, but relax and allow Spirit to work within you. Listen to your thoughts. Listen to the voice of your heart. Transcribe what your feelings offer. It is the source of Spirit Light.

Perhaps at the end of the day before you retire, reflect on your day's activities, and write down your thoughts and aspirations. Regardless of who you are, remember that the Creator loves you as a child. Remember that there is much admiration from the heavenly host for all your efforts, in whatever you do. Remember that it takes time and patience to achieve. The Creator knows this Truth and recognizes your strengths and weakness and loves you without condition or expectation. You are not judged but accepted fully. Each effort you make, however small, regardless of whether it is perceived as a success, brings so much happiness in the spiritual realm. Untold joy abounds everywhere as you choose this path of Light.

Here is an exercise that will assist you. At the end of each year you may choose to pen your aspirations for the next year. In subsequent years, you can review your progress. It is a wonderful way to count your blessings. Know that it is Truth that you will see your blessings multiply. Do the same each day and each week and each month.

Remember always that you are deeply loved regardless of your past, present or future. You are loved regardless of what you have accomplished. Remember that the simple act of keeping a journal is one step achieved. Realize that you are progressing. Always remember that you are so deeply loved and cherished. Accept this Love.

In journaling, it is a good idea to include the date, time and place of each entry. It can serve as a powerful log of your life. For example, if you go to Disneyland, you could include words about the joy of being there, and lessons that you have learned from the places and the new people you meet.

You may also include dreams in your journal. Remember to note that it was a dream, and again include the date, time and place. Here, whatever is received must be written. This is an exception to the suggestion of including only the positive. Dreams should be entered upon rising and in their entirety. However, consider spending time during the day to meditate upon the dream, seeking the interpretation and messages that were offered. Perhaps by the end of the day, you will have the interpretation to add to your journal. If the interpretation does not come to you by the end of the day, then perhaps you can leave a space in your journal so that it can be added later. Interpretations do come at the most unexpected moment. As you work with your dreams, you gain experience and confidence with interpretation. It is a powerful source of guidance.

In summary, remember to find time each day, perhaps before retiring, or at sunrise or even both, to put pen to paper. Let this be a process to assist you as you seek answers. Allow only the positive to fall on to the paper, and let the wind take the rest.

(a) How do you feel about the day's activities and achievements? Identify areas that require improvement. Establish a plan for improvement. Perhaps write about attitudes and emotions that will assist with plans for the next day.

(b) What are your aspirations for tomorrow? What are your aspirations for this year? What are your aspirations for this life?

(c) Did you have dreams? What are the interpretations of the dreams?

(d) You may seek ways to create joy in your life. You may seek processes to create a clear conscience.

(e) You may seek ways to manifest the Creator's Love more effectively. You may seek ways to express the Creator's Love. You may seek ways to manifest your Love without condition or expectation. You may seek ways to learn how to accept without judgment.

(f) Transcribe the words shared by Spirit.

(g) Write about your plans to manifest Love and Truth.

(h) Write about ways to achieve oneness with Spirit.

(i) Write about taking command of the totality of your being.

(j) Write about responding to life with your Spirit and heart.

These are only a few ideas, but allow Spirit from within to be the guide. Remember that life consists of many small steps taken with patience.

Life does offer many opportunities, and this is a wonderful channel of growth. You will be amazed when you read your journal in the future, and realize the vast changes which you have embraced in your lifetime. You will appreciate that your life is blessed. You will understand the power of choice. You will realize the amazing power within your command.

As you embark on this journey, feel the warmth and Love of the Creator of life within you. Feel the many blessings of the heavenly host that embrace you on your journey onward and upward into Light. Amen.

Reflection

The Oak

Mighty and tall
Planted firmly in the ground
Withstands the wind
Withstands the rain
Withstands the snow

Grows upward to the sky
Bears seed
And creates once more
The oak

Mighty and tall
Planted firmly in Truth
Withstands the challenges of the ego
Withstands the challenges of pride
Withstands the temptations of the flesh
Withstands the lure of the world

Being in command
Manifesting Love
Manifesting Truth
Being the example

Creating in the flesh
All that is Spirit.
Amen.

Lesson 33

The Journey of Rituals

It is paramount to always maintain a strong connection between Spirit and the flesh. In your journey through existence, you face new challenges every day. As you travel to new places and meet new people, you must realize that the flesh seeks the path of survival. It is important to maintain the connection with Spirit to manifest the Spirit in Love and Truth in every moment.

How do you do this? How do you keep this connection strong? Perhaps it will become easier as you grow and your consciousness expands to embrace all that you are. However, you need to do what is necessary to transcend the pathway of survival and open the doorway of the Spirit and keep it open.

The Native peoples of America and around the world use rituals. Most religions do. Over time, however, the true purpose of these rituals became lost.

Some pray. Some meditate. Some read sacred writings. Some use music, drums, chanting and dancing. Some use drugs to induce euphoric states. In ancient Chinese tradition, the monks in conjunction with their spiritual teachings used mastering of the body through physical training such as kung fu. Some used rituals of prayer and meditation synchronized with the intersection of time with the Light of the sun, moon and stars. Although some may forget the purpose, all have been originally designed to reawaken and strengthen in some form or fashion, a connection between Spirit and the flesh.

On a personal path of growth, you sometimes find certain activities that aid with the opening of the doorway between Sprit and flesh. You can choose to use these when needed. It is easy to become distracted by the physical senses and the wants of the flesh, especially on the path of physical survival. It is so easily forgotten that you are truly Spirit manifesting in flesh. Said in a different way, it is easy to forget that the flesh is simply a temple or house for Spirit to manifest in the physical realm. The rituals that support this connection and reinforce it are important in maintaining this awareness, so the connection with your true being is strengthened. It is the key to spiritual growth.

When you choose to walk onward, and you have chosen that pathway of joy and fulfillment, a path of Love and Truth, it is a pathway where flesh and Spirit unite as one. It is the path where you become a warrior of Light. When you embrace the source of your strength and nourish yourself spiritually, mentally and physically, you will become a victor in the battle of life in which your Spirit has conquered the flesh.

Reflection

To Stand in Your Power

Let your heart grow strong.
Let your Spirit grow strong.

Grow strong in courage.
Shine your Light from within.

Honour your heart.
Honour the Truth.
Honour all that you are.

Shine as Spirit manifesting in the flesh,
For you are a Light being.

Stand firm for all that you are.
Stand firm for all that is.
It is your power.
Amen.

Meditation

Posture

Stand with Love.
Stand with Truth.
Stand with Spirit.
Stand with Light.
Stand with God.
Amen.

Reflection

The Ritual of Food

In ancient times, humans walked into this realm and walked back out at will. The physical body experienced only that which was chosen. The body was guided by Spirit, and not by the appetites of the mind.

Food was not necessary, except for the experience. This experience created genetic structures for digesting the meat. Food then became necessary for a body that was earthbound.

To separate the need for food and the experience of food is truly a challenge that requires much commitment. Spirit is aware of your physical needs and the sacred path back to the ethereal existence.

Before taking food, one who walks the sacred path first takes the time to meditate, seeking guidance and directing the body to assimilate what is needed to manifest the desires of the Spirit.

Spiritual sustenance before physical, thus take time to meditate before each meal.

Illumination

The Word Made Flesh

It is your very core, your essence, your Spirit.
It is who you are.

No one can take it away from you,
Unless you choose to give it away.

Manifest Truth, your core, your Spirit.
Manifest your essence.

Transcend fear.
Transcend judgment.
Take command of your being.

The control of the mind has lost its sting.

Let the Light of the Spirit shine from your very core.
Know who you are.

You are Truth.
Let your word be Truth.

Let your word be the Light of your Spirit.
Let your word be the essence of your being.

Have the courage to be the Light that you are
And shine from the place of Spirit within,
The word made flesh.
Amen.

Lesson 34

Finding a Rainbow

The start of each new year ushers in changes which impact the Earth, world events, humanity and the individual. It can be viewed as a cycle of time and space, the cycle of being at the same place over and over again. It is the way of creation offering remembrance through a recurring path of awakening.

Although time cycles exist, Truth will reveal that nothing exists beyond this moment. The conundrum lies only within the mind; thus, the perception creates the reality. When you stop and put aside the yearning of the mind, Truth in its purest form becomes present in the consciousness. Meditation is a tool that can be used to open this door. Realize that Spirit knows and sees all. Spirit existed in the beginning. Spirit offers such Truth to the mind; however, the consciousness is only aware of what the mind is willing to see and accept.

The mind is also aware of what it has experienced through physical senses in its lifetime. If life is based on the capacities of the mind such as reason and judgment, it becomes limited by those boundaries. However, existence, which is based on the capacities of the Spirit, is unlimited. The mind is only a tool. It can be used for many purposes. Spirit can use it as a tool for growth.

As you grow, you will understand that existence extends beyond the boundaries of the mind. Existence is sometimes described as a duality, having a physical and spiritual component. From one perspective, this is correct, but from another, Spirit extends into the physical. Thus, all of existence is one, and the perception of duality is simply an illusion created by the mind to form boundaries for its survival.

You have an awareness of the relationship between the mind

and your physical existence. It is based on the survival of the physical body as perceived by physical senses. Spirit, however, will navigate you along a different path, one which leads to the totality of existence. The totality of all of existence can be perceived as the Creator of life or God. [seventh chakra]

Once you can accept this Truth, you will understand that the essence of life is eternal and the flesh is only a cocoon, a phase in your experience. You can learn how to fly free, independent of the physical. With this awareness and experience, you can prepare for the next phase on the journey upward and onward into totality.

Once you gain your wings of freedom from the flesh, what will you do with them? It is Truth that you are never without guidance. All you need is always with you. You need only open your eyes, Spirit eyes, and you will see the wonders that surround you.

As you study the chakra system as presented in this book, you will learn that the third, which resonates with the vibration of yellow, is a place where challenges originate. It is true that all the chakras work hand in hand as a unit, each with its unique purpose, each awakening at different times and called upon when needed to perform a unique purpose, which is to aid with the embrace of totality. The seventh chakra is your connection with Spirit. The ancients have seen this as a white glow that surround the head.

In the same way that the chakras work together as one, you will see that all of humanity is connected as one, and all life is connected as one, corpuscles within the body of existence, each with an individual and unique purpose and place in the totality of life, indeed a spark of the Creator of life.

When you choose, you exercise your free will, independence and uniqueness. It is that part of your being that is connected to the totality of existence. Each life holds a place in the "network" of reality. Choice manifests your purpose and place in this totality. The freedom to choose is the essence of your being. It is your birthright. It is the spark of your being that is the image of all life.

If you accept God, the Creator of life, as the totality of existence, it is easy to see that you are part of God, and you hold a spark of God's Light within. On the journey of life, you choose to embody this totality here in the physical realm. When Light is split, as seen in the rainbow, it brings the remembrance of whom you truly are. Each colour represents a part and component of your being. You have seen that the third chakra spins with yellow; the sixth, indigo, and so on. When you experience all the colours, it is the expression of your Spirit sparkling in oneness with your physicality. Spirit is Love and its expression glows with green, gold, purple and white. To embrace the totality of your being, the brilliance of your rainbow, Light will shine from the centre of your being, filling your aura with a rainbow of colours.

Let the rainbow be a symbol to remind you that you are a being of Light shining from far beyond into the realm of the physical. Refer to the Book of Genesis, chapter 9, verses 9-16 of the King James Version of the Bible. As time cycles, and as you make resolutions for each new year, set your sight on the totality of your being by choosing to embrace all that you are. Shine with all the colours of the rainbow. Let the rainbow in the sky serve as a guide to the rainbow within, which is the fabric and totality of your being. Amen.

Reflection

Do You Know Who You Are?

Some time ago, a man was guided to fast for forty days. He found that the benefits were truly amazing, physically and more so, spiritually.

One day during the fast, as he rested his weary body, he felt hunger pangs. The thought of food filled him, but his disciplined mind excluded any possibility of allowing himself to eat anything. As he settled down for the rest that his body needed, he felt a presence beside him, looking down upon him and communicating with him. It was uncomfortable. The presence lacked definition. Its energy felt grey and muddy, with dull red in the neck area. It was large and clothed in rags. There was a message. The man was told that he had won that battle this time, but he would not win the war.

The man realized that it was an energy seeking to manifest within him its desire to experience food. It was seeking to exploit his hunger in the moment. The energy felt defeated but was not willing to give up the fight.

The man understood that appetites and desires can originate from external forces. He realized that he has the choice to give it expression, or reject it.

As he meditated, he appreciated that life is Light, manifested as Love and Truth and its expression creates joy. It is through choice in each moment and such situations that one can manifest Love and Truth.

Reflection

Wait Upon the Spirit

The mind seeks to create.
But I say unto you, wait on the words of Spirit.
Spirit will emerge and bring you guidance.
Recognize Spirit.

Love.
Truth.
Joy.
Light.
Life.

Reflection

Earth

She is gentle and kind.
Patient in every way.
Smiling each morning with her warmth.
Clothing you.
Feeding you.
Housing you.
Washing away your sorrows with her tears.
Loving you as she shares her body.
Looking after your every need.

She responds to your Love with growth.
She responds to your kindness with stability.
She responds to your care with abundance.
She responds to harmony with gentleness.
She responds to peace with calm.
She responds to your smile with beauty.

She responds to your body.
She responds to your mind.
She responds to your Spirit.
She responds to your state of being.

Know the Truth
For she seeks balance
As she reflects what you hold in your heart.
Amen.

Lesson 35

Shine in Your Brilliance

You are energy. You are a being of Light. Let your Light shine. Expose yourself. Be all that you are.

You no longer need to hide your Love. You no longer need to hide your Truth. You no longer need to hide your heart. It is by choice that you have created the proverbial bushel under which you shield yourself. It is your choices, one at a time, that have brought you to this place where you are here and now.

You can, if you will, follow the pathway navigated by choice, back to where you once stood in your brilliance. It is your choices that will once again remove the bushel, one challenge at a time, one victory at a time, back to the place of brilliance.

Yes, you are the creator of your being. All that you are is a result of your choice, will and power. Release yourself from the prison which now holds you where you are. [Seed: Meditate upon this statement.] Make new choices, which will unlock the chains that bind your energy, and open the door to freedom where you can shine once more in your brilliance.

Meditation

I Live

I live with the guidance of Spirit.
I live; therefore, "I AM."

I live with the will to manifest Truth.
I live upon the bread of life.
I live to choose a new path.
I live to create new life.
I live with Love.
Amen.

Reflection

I Live Again

From earth to life
From dust to breath
The ashes rise up once more.

Here to stand in the Light
The yarns of Love to weave
The yarns of Truth to sew.

Creating joy.
Shining.

Prayer

Return

I seek your protection
Here in this realm
That you may walk beside me
Shielding me with your golden light.

Now
And as I journey onward
Guide me
Bless me
Heal me
Teach me
Strengthen me.

And for all this
I give thanks.
Amen.

Chapter Five

Karma and Forgiveness

Introduction

It takes strength and courage to choose wisely and fulfill your purpose for being here in this realm. In meditation, the dichotomy of flesh and Spirit ends, revealing your essence, as it was in the beginning. The time line of existence is scattered with attitudes and patterns, which the ancient teachers described as karma. Some patterns serve the Spirit while others do not. The persona that Spirit seeks to manifest existed in the beginning before the onset of karma. The persona that the Spirit seeks is veiled by karma.

Karmic patterns are awakened by emotions and are the key to transformation. Recognizing the patterns, which no longer serve the Spirit, are opportunities to choose differently, thereby opening the door to transformation.

You exercised free will from the start of your journey into physicality. It is choice that navigated you to the present. Likewise, choice will guide you on the return journey of freedom from karma.

The fabric of reality is woven with Truth. It is Love which gives life to your creation. Choice is the power to manifest your desire. Desire is the fundamental essence and function of Spirit. Joy is the nature of Spirit. Allow your meditative insights to guide you as you set about weaving a new reality.

Forgiveness

Where is life? It is neither yesterday nor tomorrow, but in the very moment you pause to take a breath. From the perspective of Spirit, life is but a single moment expanded to embrace all. Within this moment, time is only an illusion. From the perspective of the mind, each lifetime is but a series of moments.

It is the intention of Spirit to journey back to the moment of totality. Your return journey will be filled with challenges. Hardships will evolve out of the karmic ties you have created in the past. Hardships are simply opportunities to end old patterns by choosing differently in the moment. Victory means the embrace of your totality and an end to the cycle of re-birth into this realm.

Karma and temptation can be viewed as the same. Old patterns emerge in the form of temptation. You feel enticed to move in a certain direction. The "debts," as found in the fifth line of "*The Prayer to Our Father,*" or connections you established with others in the past resurface, offering the opportunity to restructure the relationship and your being, building upon a foundation of Love and Truth. The restructuring process will require acceptance without condition and judgment. It will require accepting the equality of mankind, womankind and children-kind. It will require living the Truth where no one is greater or lesser. It will require the transforming energy of forgiveness.

What is forgiveness? It is threefold. It is forgiving, being forgiven and accepting forgiveness. Forgiveness lies on the pathway to the end of karma. Much like medicine, which cures diseases, forgiveness, which comes from the Spirit, holds a transforming power over the one who forgives and also the forgiven. You need to experience this to realize the power at your command.

When you forgive, do it quickly and earnestly. Do not wait

until tomorrow. When you feel you have been judged unjustly, always be prepared to forgive from the depths of your being.

Acceptance without condition, expectation or judgment is the key, for in Truth, acceptance is forgiveness. Set an example by being quick to forgive fully and completely and even quicker to forget.

Even more difficult is the ability to forgive self and accept forgiveness from others. Forgiveness is acceptance, and to accept the self unconditionally and without judgment is the foundation of Love. To love oneself completely is the beginning of freedom. Meditation and guidance from Spirit will help with all these challenges.

Meditate upon the meaning of forgiveness. Realize that it is not simply the utterance of words. Words can be empty. Forgiveness goes deeper and requires a change in attitude. It is borne out of the tempering energy flowing from the fourth chakra. What flows from the fourth chakra? It is the transforming power of Love. The transforming power of Love is forgiveness out of which emerges a new path, a new direction or a new choice.

When there is division, anger or pain, out of each situation there is an opportunity for a lesson. If the situation cannot be totally dissolved and forgotten, let the lesson not become a scar of remembrance, but instead an opportunity to forge the bonds of Love, friendship and acceptance. Remember, to forgive is a mighty challenge and accepting forgiveness is even mightier.

Sparkle with the energy that flows from the fourth chakra, tempering the activities of the third and fill your aura with such brilliance, always be quick to forgive and even quicker to accept forgiveness.

When Forgiveness Fails

If you feel the desired result of forgiveness is not being achieved, and you are being persistently offended, then such an environment is not beneficial for your journey onward into Light. Under such circumstances, you need to choose a different path, one where there is creativity, mutual acceptance, where judgment ends and there is Love and the desire for true joy. All these exist in an environment of true forgiveness.

Look in the Mirror

You are much like a mirror. The best teacher is this mirror! It is learning through observation and embracing those patterns desired by Spirit.

Those who are impressionable may subconsciously emulate you. When you forgive, others learn forgiveness. Others assume your pattern of accepting forgiveness. Others realize that they also become the examples of forgiving and accepting forgiveness. It is the cycle of universal Love. Embrace this lesson as you allow the true teacher from within to emerge.

Observation is a two-edged sword which carves opportunities not only for others, but for self. As you observe others, you gain the opportunity to reap life lessons. For example, when the mind judges another, realize that it is simply looking in a mirror observing parts of the self, hidden deep within. It is an opportunity not only to express Love and acceptance for others, but to embrace the self with Love and acceptance. It is an opportunity to address the hidden self by choosing differently in the moment, thereby restructuring the foundation of your own being.

Observation is a powerful tool to be used in every moment. Step aside and look at the situation. Step aside and look at yourself. The body is a tool used by the Spirit to experience the fullness of life. It is the tool which creates karma. It is the same tool which can be used to end karma. By being a channel of forgiveness through the power of Love and Truth, you can end karma. Such is the way of healing self and others.

For example, what opportunities can a body that is challenged physically or mentally offer? The ability to step aside and observe provides the opportunity to dissolve karma, both for self and others. The mind will seek control. Although the mind will fight to remain in control, you have the power to choose differently. You can choose the path of Love, which is the acceptance of self without condition or judgment. Choose to manifest these strengths, as you are guided by your Spirit from within and let it be an opportunity for ending karma.

Always be prepared to face the challenges that your karma offers. If you find yourself in a position of power over others, perhaps as a leader, teacher, parent, guide or elder, how will you manifest this power? Will you choose the way of control for self-aggrandizement or the way of Love and Truth by being a living example? Listen for the guidance of your Spirit that flows from within, and you will hear the words of Love and Truth.

When you exercise your power to choose Love and Truth, you are weaving a strong fabric that will carry you through difficult situations, even if the body and mind are challenged. As you journey, the flesh may grow weak and fade, but the Spirit is strong with the will to sustain you to the very end. The power of Spirit is far beyond what the mind can imagine. Move onward with the faith that there is life beyond what can be seen by the mind, and by ending karma, you will open a door to this reality that is known only by Spirit. It is one that embraces eternal joy.

Embark on this journey beyond the limits of the mind. Karma forms the substance of the mind and requires observation to transcend its limits onto the eternal.

Balance

Observation requires balance. If you find that you are not in balance, find the reason and address it quickly. In each moment, choose to observe the Light, which you shine. What do you see? Is it the pure clear Light of your Spirit that embraces all and touches all with Love and joy? What do you need to do to shine with such brilliance? When Spirit is in command, manifesting Love and Truth, you are in balance and shine with that pure clear Light. Embrace this Truth, as you grow spiritually on your journey onward and upward, shining with brilliance.

Channelling

As you grow spiritually, you can allow energies from the realms beyond to use your body as an instrument for channelling their Love and Truth. Realize that Love extends to every corner of existence and is not limited by the boundaries of space and time. It is not limited by the mind. Many from the realms beyond are desperately seeking to share their Love and Truth and await your invitation. By the stepping aside of your physicality, you can allow those energies to use your body as a means of communication.

If you choose to be a channel, then prepare yourself by fully and clearly defining your aspirations. Invite only those who align with your aspirations. Enter the gates of sharing with an expectancy of the purest and deepest Love and Truth.

Healing

Spirit will communicate in many ways and at many levels. You can choose the method. By observing your thoughts, feelings, emotions and inner sight, you can become aware of their presence. You can become aware of the Love and Truth that is being offered. Spirit offers a healing Light by impressing its energy upon your physicality. Observation allows you to receive the Truth, which opens the door to manifest this healing energy.

When you choose to use your physicality as a channel for Spirit, go beyond the illusion of this physical world and find what is real. Find Spirit. Always choose Love and Truth to be your guide and protector. Hold tight to the fabric with which you have been created as you journey into this Light.

Spirit or Flesh

Yesterday, today and evermore you are and shall be a result of choice, which evolves and has evolved from your totality, for you are on that ever-seeking path of spiritual brilliance. King or pauper, strong or lame, brilliant or maimed, sorrowful or loved, joyous or warring, the objective of the Spirit remains the same. The attitudes and emotions are the same. Love is the same. Truth is the same. The challenge of choice is the same. The spiritual joy you experience is the same. The rainbow of Light, which is your spiritual brilliance, is also the same. Do not be deceived by inequalities seen by flesh eyes, treasures that fade with time, beauty that ends when you grow old or the illusion of power over the masses.

Understand your urges, feelings and desires. What is the source? What is their purpose? How do you manifest them? When faced with a challenge, will you choose between the way of the Spirit or the aggrandizement of self? These are the two paths that challenges offer. The simple path is the way of the flesh, such as seeking control or power over another. You have been there before. Circumstances may be new, but the principles of the challenge remain the same. The emotions are the same. The patterns are part of your being and challenges are borne out of your conscious memory or cellular memory so you may gain the opportunity to forge a new way.

The difficult path is always the way of the Spirit, where you end old patterns and establish new ones. It may take you on a new pathway where you could lose friends, family, jobs or find yourself in a different part of the world. You will be faced with many new emotions that you once avoided. You will be faced with many fears that you have previously circumvented. You will be stepping out of the comfort zone created by the mind. When this occurs, reason, a tool of the flesh, will seek to defy the way of the Spirit.

Glowing with Yellow

Realize that you have the power to transcend old patterns. You have the power to overcome the illusion of fear and discover the joys that lie beyond its boundaries. You have the power to experience the joys of new emotions. You have the power to overcome what you perceive as hurdles. You have the power to become a living example of all that is Love and Truth.

This power comes from the energy that flows from the third chakra, seen in the aura as a brilliant yellow glow. With every breath you take, the transforming power of the Creator of life flows down through the crown to the third chakra. Your decision-making becomes a dance of colour as your energy expands and glows with a brilliant yellow.

Change

This is the time, and this is the moment. Just do it. You are the commander of your being. To affect change in your life, you need to take action. "The buck stops here." For too long you have suffered within a cyclic framework of submission, continually giving, continually yielding. You are worthy of joy. You are worthy of your desires. You are worthy of Love. You are worthy of acceptance. You are worthy of all the fullness that life offers. It is time to end the judgment. It is time to cross the boundaries and limitations of fear. You are a being of Love and Truth. Your very essence is Love and Truth. You have validity. It is time to restore your self-worth. It is time to change, and as commander of your being, you need to take action. There is no better time than now.

Third Chakra Meditation

The purpose of this meditation is to harmonize body, mind and Spirit and expand the energy of the third chakra. The aura this energy radiates is a brilliant yellow.

As you meditate, focus on the area of the third chakra. The symbol to hold in your mind is "debt." This chakra corresponds with the adrenal glands, located in the solar plexus.

As this area becomes active, cellular memory or karma is awakened through challenges that were seeded in this lifetime or beyond. You face challenges of the flesh. You face challenges that arise from the connection you hold with others. As you meditate, contemplate the acceptance of self and others. Contemplate forgiveness. Contemplate the pathway of Love, which flows from above, the area of the fourth chakra, tempering your choices and activities. Contemplate the way of Truth that flows from the area of the fifth chakra. Contemplate the way of the Spirit, which flows from the sixth and seventh chakra. As the energy of the chakras stirs within you, it flows up and down, pouring from the crown all the way to the base or root chakra.

Your life energy stirs within your being, described by the ancient teachers as the awakening of the "kundalini." (Because of what you may feel within your physicality, it is sometimes confused as sexual energy.) Allow this energy to rise to the third chakra. Transform this energy within the third chakra. It holds the blueprint of life. It holds the pattern of Love and Truth. As your karma unfolds, transform this energy by embracing its power to create the life you choose, thereby manifesting the desires of the Spirit.

With each challenge, by choosing the way of Spirit, you will unlock the karmic ties. By embracing challenges with Love, you will be one step closer to the door of freedom from this realm. In this meditation, embrace your power to choose the way of the Spirit, establishing new patterns in all your interactions.

When the third chakra is in balance, when you are empowered by the Light, when you are in command of your being, the energy fills your aura with a brilliant yellow glow.

Prayer
As you prepare for meditation, take time to pray. Seek the guidance and protection offered by the Light of the Creator. Know your aspirations. Let your intentions manifest your aspirations. Let Spirit be the source of power behind your intentions. Embrace the Light you feel within and around you.

Connecting with the Light
In this meditation, you will have the opportunity to explore your connection with the Light to become empowered to manifest the Truth and Love you hold within. There is much to gain as you learn how to recognize this connection. You will find that it is a source of guidance for the journey onward and upward into Light.

There is much Love and Truth that awaits your command. In this meditation, you will embrace this connection and open yourself to the source of all Love and Truth.

Light Meditation
Find a comfortable position, spine gently erect, and relax. Take three gentle breaths, slowly, continuously and connectedly, and allow the Spirit of relaxation to permeate your body. Allow the Spirit of Love to fill your heart. Allow the Spirit of Truth to expand and touch every cell within your being. As you breathe, feel the flow of energy within your body.

With your eyes closed, take a gentle breath, and as you exhale, relax. Feel the gentleness of your Spirit. Feel the quietness seep into every cell of your body. Feel the silence as it trickles into your mind.

Take a deep and gentle breath, and as you exhale, release all attachments that call for the attention of your mind, one at a time, allowing the silence to go even deeper. Be here and now. Be in this moment. Be as silent as the Light you feel within you. Let every cell of your being rest in this silence.

As the Nazarene Master commanded the storm in the Book of Mark chapter 4, verse 39 of the King James Version of the Bible, command also your mind. "Peace, be still." Know who you are. Your Spirit is Light. Know that you are Light. You are the enlightened one.

You have the free will to choose. You have the power to choose. From the depths of your silence, choose the way of freedom offered by the Spirit. Realize that your Spirit is free to Love. Spirit is Love.

Realize that Spirit is Truth, unchangeable and unmovable. Realize that you are Truth.

Take a deep, deep breath. As you exhale, allow your being to be filled with the Light flowing from above. You are a being of Light, with wings to soar above the call of the flesh, above the call of your physicality, above the lure of this realm. As you shine, take a moment to reach out to the all-embracing Light, in prayer.

Prayer

The voice of my Spirit reaches out to the realms of Love and Truth and Light as I prepare my heart, my mind, my being, to enter the silence of meditation. Open the doorway of my consciousness so I may partake of all the Love and Truth that is the foundation of reality. Surround my being with the Light of protection that I may be touched only by the Love and Truth that shines from the realms of the Creator of life. Amen.

Healing Rain-Guided Imagery

Take a deep and gentle breath, and as you exhale, feel the stillness of Spirit within. Feel that gentle quietness within the Light you see within, for it is your Spirit.

Feel that peace within like a gentle rain. Stand in the rain and feel the droplets, bathing your entire being with soothing warmth. Give yourself permission to go further into a state of deep relaxation. With the calming touch of each gentle droplet of healing balm, feel every muscle find rest and comfort, from the crown of your head all the way to the soles of your feet.

Feel the energy within each droplet of rain permeate your body, touching every cell, transforming, cleansing, purifying, nourishing and surrounding each cell with healing energy.

Feel the revitalization of your energy centres, expanding and working in unison. As the cleansing and life-giving warmth of the rain droplets invigorate each cell of your being, feel the power of transformation fill your being. Feel the Light within. Feel this Light grow brighter. Feel the enlightenment within the totality of your being.

Feel the transforming power embrace your third chakra. Feel the oneness with all life, as the doorway of Truth opens to reveal all that you are, past, present and future. It is a doorway that offers transformation. Enter the gates of your consciousness filled with Love, armed with acceptance that holds no condition or judgment of self and all others.

Prayer

Divine Creator, I pray that you fill me with such power that I may enter the gates of my consciousness with acceptance, without condition and without judgment, that I may journey along the path of transformation filled with strength and courage, to the place of harmony where Spirit embraces the flesh as one. Amen.

In this place of silence, as your consciousness expands to embrace all, look within. Here you will see all that you are. You will see all your sojourns, past and present. You will become aware of your attachments, old patterns and belief structures. Here you will see what serves and what no longer serves Spirit.

Enter these gates with acceptance of all that you are. It is a time to transcend all judgments. It is time to allow the transforming energy of Truth to embrace you.

Take a gentle and deep breath, and as you slowly exhale, focus on the area of the third chakra. Feel your consciousness expand to unconditionally embrace all that you are.

Take a gentle and deep breath, and as you slowly exhale, become aware of your feelings.

Take a gentle and deep breath, and as you slowly exhale, become aware of your attachments.

Take a gentle and deep breath, and as you slowly exhale, become aware of your belief structures.

With the transforming energy of the fourth chakra, there is no judgment, only acceptance.

As each feeling, each attachment, each belief structure emerges, embrace them with Love.

With each breath, explore the totality of your being, knowing that you are loved fully and completely by the angels and the Creator of life. You are being observed by the Creator of life and by a host of angels, with Love and admiration.

You are accepted without condition or judgment by the Creator of life and by the angels. Likewise, Love and accept yourself. It is the way of healing and transformation.

Accept the patterns, belief structures and attachments that serve the Spirit. Allow all others to be washed away by the gentle rain that falls as droplets of Love from the Creator's Light. Accept this healing from the Creator of life.

[Pause]

Healing Light-Guided Imagery

Feel the Light of the Creator like the golden sun that rises in the east, melting away the darkness of the night. Allow that crimson morning Light to bathe your entire being with warmth, dissolving all that no longer serves your Spirit.

Know that you are loved. Know that you are Love. Feel every fibre of your being dance with Light. Feel the warmth of the crimson sunrise fill your being, your consciousness. Feel every cell dance with the transforming Light. Feel every cell dance as they shine with the Light of Love.

[Pause]

As the Light fills the sky, the trees and the forest, life emerges everywhere. The morning Light brings joy to life. Listen to the music of the wind in the leaves, and birds as the day awakens.

In Spirit, all things are possible. Travel now in Spirit, like the eagle, high up to the place where the sun meets the sky. In the distance, there is a forest. Let your Spirit travel to that forest.

Walk through the lush green forest. There is a special place, one that you know quite well. It is the place where you often go when you contemplate, to be alone and serene. No one knows of this place except you. Here you can feel the silence, undisturbed by the world. Find your favourite place, a patch of soft grass, and lie upon your back looking up through the trees and leaves. Feel the Light of the sun filtering down through the leaves, sprinkling upon your face, dancing and shimmering. It is truly your sanctuary, your place of total freedom.

It is your place of silent reflection where you are alone with your thoughts and feelings. It is a place of inspiration, where you gather Truth to guide you through life. Indeed, it is where you commune with the realms beyond and meet with the angels and your guides. Here, you listen to the music of the realms and embrace the Love and Truth, which flow from the heart of the Creator of life.

You are in Spirit, free of the body and mind, free of the flesh. Your eyes open to the nakedness of Truth, life and Love, and your totality. Feel the purity of life. Feel and absorb the energy that surrounds you. Allow this transforming energy to touch every cell of your being.

Take time to feel the rhythm of your heart, for it is the rhythm of life. It is the rhythm of Love. Listen to the beat of Love. Take the time to feel the Love you hold within. Embrace the Love offered from the realms beyond. Unite as one with this Love, knowing that you are Love.

Take the time to feel Truth within your being. Take the time to listen for the voice of Truth spoken from within your heart. Embrace the Truth offered from the realms beyond. Unite as one with Truth, for you are Truth.

The healing Light is filtering down from above, bathing your entire being. Take a gentle breath and allow this Light to fill your entire being. As you breathe, feel this Light permeate every cell, knowing that it is the transforming Light from the Creator of life. Become one with the Light of the Creator flooding your being. You are enlightened.

[Pause]

Know from the very core of your being that you are all that you are. You are Love. You are Truth. You are kind. You are gentle. You are the manifestation of peace. Indeed, you are Light.

Take time to experience the freedom from the flesh. Receive all that is offered by the Light. Receive all that is needed by the flesh. Receive all that is desired by the Spirit. This is the time. This is the place. Fill your being with the knowingness that your life in this very moment is sharing oneness with all of life, for life is Light and you are one with all that is Light.

Change

Fill yourself with the knowingness that you are the commander of your being. You are the commander of your totality. Embrace your power to choose. Embrace your power to take action; action that will affect change; action that will manifest your desires; action that will restore your validity. You are Love and worthy of Love. It is your action that will manifest this Truth. It is your action that will manifest your desires. It is your action that will manifest change.

Embrace your power to take action.

Embrace your power to affect change.

Embrace your power to bring joy into your being.

[Pause]

You have triumphed.

You are filled with joy.

The angels dance in celebration.

Dance with the angels.

[Pause]

It is time to bid farewell and return to your physicality. Before you leave the realm of Light, take the opportunity to give thanks for all that you have received. Give thanks to the angels. Give thanks to your teachers and guides. Give thanks to the Creator of life. Seek wisdom, guidance and strength for your journey onward.

It is time to travel back through the forest, into the sunshine, the rain, to the place where you started.

Feeling transformed and renewed by the Light of the Spirit, you take a gentle breath, and as you exhale, allow your consciousness to return to the physical realm, embracing your mind and body.

Feeling empowered to command your being, empowered to affect change, feeling totally refreshed, alert, loved and healed, you gently open your eyes.

Amen.

Prayer of Light

I give thanks for Light that is life.

I give thanks for healing.

I give thanks for the harmony it brings to my life.

I give thanks for harmony that I can radiate.

I give thanks for the power to radiate a rainbow of Love and Light, as I journey onward, along the path of life.

Amen.

Prayer of Thanks

I give thanks for this time of meditation.

I give thanks for the peace and Love and Truth that were shared.

I give thanks for the healing, and pray that these blessings remain with me as I journey onward through life.

I give thanks to my guides and teachers.

I give thanks to all who inspire me to embrace Truth.

I give thanks to the angels.

I give thanks to the legions that protected me.

I seek the blessing of such protection and guidance as I journey onward and upward into Light.

Amen.

Reflection

Life in Its Form

In each moment
I will choose to be in command.

For it is more than my purpose.
It is being all that I am.

I will let it be my aspiration
To regain my totality.

To take back what is mine
And restore my being
To its pristine form.

Meditation

I Command

I am Spirit
Manifesting.

I am Love.
I am Truth.
I am the "I AM."
I am all that I am.

I command
All that I am.

Meditation

To Be

To embrace life
To be Love
To be Truth
To be one in Spirit and flesh
To be free
To fly free from the limits of the flesh
To accept without condition
To be the "I AM"
To be all that I am
To be in command of my totality

Illumination

Joy

Choose joy.
Create joy.
Manifest joy.
Feel joy.
Become joy.
You are joy.
Spirit is joy
You are Spirit.
Remember.

Reflection

More Joy

Take time to contemplate who you are.
Contemplate being in the state of joy.

It is an intrinsic part of your nature.
It is an intrinsic part of who you are.

You are joy.
It is your essence.

Choose joy.
Move in the direction of joy.
Embrace all that offers joy.

Let joy be your guide.

Reflection

Sailing

How do you find the Truth which life offers, and learn who you are, where you came from and where you are going? These questions have been asked throughout eternity, and today, you are still searching for the answers. With these answers, will you be able to sail effortlessly through life?

As you seek answers, you realize that you are at a point at which you have embraced a purpose, ready to move onward, but you feel that you do not know where it will lead. You feel that you are sailing blindly in uncharted waters, in need of a map and compass for navigation.

Have you ever taken the time to consider the wind? Where does it come from, and where is it going? From whose mouth did this mighty breath take flight? You may find different answers to such questions. Even the scientific community may offer what they consider absolute Truth, but within, you feel that the answers you seek remain elusive, for you realize that the physical world with all its research can offer only their perspectives.

As you sail along life's sinuous pathways without guidance, how can you know if you are travelling in the "right" direction? Ask yourself this question: How did you get where you are today? If you were asked this question ten years ago, would you know the answer? Could you say that you would be at this place here and now? Where will you find yourself physically, spiritually and mentally, ten years in the future? Can you make an accurate prediction?

As you examine your past, you realize that many of the challenges already faced would <u>not</u> have been easily accepted if you felt that you had a choice to avoid them. Nonetheless, you have gone through them and survived, and they have brought you to where you are now. Regardless of the way you feel and the challenges you anticipate, know that you are one of vast knowledge and wisdom from your past experiences.

However, the question remains: What is the purpose of being here? In times of quiet reflection in this three-dimensional world, your mind is fully capable of embracing all that is of this realm, but it takes more than the mind to embrace what is beyond. The answers which you seek are beyond this realm. What you may not realize is that you have found a source of Truth and it lies within. Meditation is the key to unlock this door.

As you change and grow and gain the realization that the understanding and wisdom you embrace today was acquired from the vast experiences throughout your lifetime, you also realize that you are truly different from who you were ten years ago. Today you are prepared for more difficult challenges. You are stronger, more powerful and courageous. The challenges of the past brought wisdom, strength and courage.

How can you account for the wind that blew you here and the compass that navigated your course?

Yes, life has it challenges. It has its ups and downs. You are swayed back and forth by the winds of change. You face stormy seas. You feel your stomach churn, and you are ready to spew its contents. You feel weak, unprepared, lacking sea legs.

When you contemplate the beauty of the sky and nature, you appreciate that there is Love and hope and peace, open to all. What is truly important is found within. You gain an understanding of your Spirit, your true being and your relationship with all of life, with Light, and indeed with the Creator of life. You look up to the sky and feel the glory of all of existence. You gain the realization that the touch of the Creator of life is in all, even within your humble bones.

Like your bones, which give your physicality form and structure, it is your Spirit which gives your life its form and structure. From whose mouth did this breath take flight? It is from your very own Spirit that seeks to guide you to the Light. It is your choice that navigated you to this place, and your choice will navigate you once again to the Light, which your Spirit seeks.

Your direction is navigated by choice, which emerges from your Spirit and is felt within your heart. You feel this direction within the voice of your own conscience. You feel this direction in your innate desire to embrace the state of spiritual joy.

What would you choose as you sail along the pathways of life? Choose joy and it will point your compass towards the Light. Indeed, your compass is activated by spiritual joy.

You have found Truth on your journey. You now know the source of Truth is within. The doorway of Truth opens as you meditate. The doorway of Truth opens when you retire to contemplate. Truth will always be your guide. Embrace the Truth which you have found. Let the compass of joy navigate you to the life you seek.

Express your thankfulness by seeking to be all that you are. Embrace all that is Truth. Embrace the Love that is eternal. Let victory be yours as you face challenges of this realm. As you sail away, choose the path of spiritual joy and journey onward and upward into Light. Amen.

Lesson 36

The Prodigal One

You are the prodigal one who has wandered far away from home, now weary, hungry and in need. The thought of your birthright and joys of your home fill you with anguish and the deep yearning to return, but you fear rejection.

Fear not, for you are already accepted. You have always been accepted. You are loved deeply, regardless of your sojourns, wherever you have been and whatever you have done. Seek and you will find, for the doorway is within. It is open: A warm welcome awaits you. You no longer need to suffer alone in emptiness.

Take up your bed and walk through this doorway of hope and return to your birthright, from where you came, a house built upon the foundation of Truth and filled with Light where you will dance in merriment from the embrace of eternal Love.

The legacy of parents is the desire to control, to mold in their image. In so doing they snuff out freedom of the Spirit to express, bringing suffering and the desire to separate from such an environment, opening the door to a wondering mind. At first, the journey of the mind can be exciting, but the joy that is founded upon material existence soon fades and the path spirals into a valley of shadows filled with disappointment, emptiness and rejection.

Realize that the path of the Spirit leads to a joy that does not fade even when material possessions diminish. It awakens the yearning to return home, to the comfort and warmth of an environment that is built upon Truth and furnished with Love.

Parents, do beware not only of your words, but your thoughts and actions, for such are the patterns embraced by the impressionable. You are the guides and Light of this realm. It is in your image that the piercing eyes of the newborn find their pattern.

Children, place not the blame upon your parents. They have brought you into this realm and offered you a framework within which you have your being. You can now manifest all that you are. All that you are is your choice, has been and always will be. Therefore, regardless of the framework that surrounds you, choose to manifest the Love and Truth which you find within and become all that you are. Amen.

Lesson 37

"Turn the Other Cheek"

What is the doctrine of acceptance? It starts at home, first with the self and expands to embrace all of life. Know that the true meaning of acceptance is Love. It is Love for self and Love for others. How do you manifest this Love? What role does it play in your purpose within this material realm? As you journey, you are faced with challenges. The self challenges you; others challenge you. What will you do when you are challenged? Are you willing to manifest the ways of your Spirit, offering yourself as an example?

Do not fear to turn the other cheek if you know that you are offering yourself to someone who needs this opportunity to find Truth within. It is an offer, so someone may gain a needed chance to open his or her eyes and heart to Truth. As you journey through this physical realm, it becomes easy to embrace its nature and become lost in its confusing reality, needing an awakening to guide you on your return journey.

The term "sacrifice" suggests depriving oneself of something. When viewed from the perspective of Spirit, it takes on a new meaning. It is a way of offering an opportunity to someone to find a connection with their Spirit within. Sacrifice may weaken the flesh, but at the same time, will strengthen the Spirit. Remember this when situations cause you to feel deprived. You enter this realm with a purpose. Have you learned your purpose? You can give thanks for the opportunities that you have been offered along the way. Likewise, you may choose to offer opportunities to others as you "turn the other cheek." As you grow in wisdom, you will realize that all of life is an opportunity and you always have the free will to choose the path that you walk.

Lesson 38

Forgiveness, a New Doctrine

What is forgiveness? The Truth of forgiveness has been lost for many in your realm, and trivialized much like the use of the word "love." Someone repeatedly offends you and you forgive over and over again because you feel that it is the nature of your spirituality. This form of forgiveness is dogma that evolved out of ancient script. Yes, forgiveness is acceptance without condition or expectation, but it goes far beyond that. It embraces the Love for self.

Life is about learning and growing through experience. To offend someone is stagnating and limits enjoyment and the opportunity for growth. It stifles your purpose for being in this realm.

If you offend someone, being repentant involves making amends. It requires a new way of being in which the offence ends. It is accepting lessons which life offers by embracing a new path.

If you were offended, when you forgive, you can expect amends and the assurance that the offence will not be repeated; otherwise, you can choose to change or end the relationship. Forgiveness is not an opportunity for martyrdom. Move out of reach of the fist. Choose to move in the direction of a creative, productive and joyous environment.

You are responsible for the totality of your being. Likewise, each individual is responsible for himself or herself. Expect no more than you are willing to give. It is easy to judge yourself harshly. It is also easy to forgive and be forgiven; however, learning from the experience is the process of growing. Learning from experience is the root of wisdom. There is growth, joy and true forgiveness in a healthy relationship.

Lesson 39

Turn the Other Cheek, a New Doctrine

Walk away! Run! Protect yourself!
Do as your heart dictates.

Ask yourself this question.
If you Love yourself, what would you do?
Then do as Love dictates,
Love for self and Love for all of humanity.
Let Truth and Love be your guide.

What do you feel is right in the moment?
This choose, then do!
Run. Walk. Stand back out of reach.
A soft answer may turn away wrath.

Do you feel that you are invited?
Do you choose to accept?
Let your heart be your guide.
Know that Truth comes from within.

Rely on the source of your life,
Your inner guidance,
Truth,
Your essence,
Your Spirit.
Amen.

Reflection

Awaken from Sleep

I looked in the mirror and what did I see? I saw Truth. Was it really me? What happened? How did I get here? What I saw came as quite a surprise! How do I return to the reality that is the true desire of my heart?

We look at the world and see the changes. Weep for the poor. Weep for the sick. Weep for the war-torn countries. Our hearts bleed for the earthquake victims. We groan at the controls that governments impose. We groan at the brain-washing antics of industry. We groan as we see our freedoms slowly erode. We look at life and feel we know what is happening. In Truth, do we really know?

What has happened to our world? What has happened to me? What do I see when I look in the mirror? Is it someone I know? Is it truly me? I do not know!

What does it take to open my eyes? What does it take to bring me to a realization that there is a greater Truth? How do I learn the Truth about the one I see before me in the mirror?

The world has changed. It is true. But how much have I changed?

Am I willing to see this change? Do I have the courage to face my own jaded reality?

Today someone asked for help. It wasn't a beggar, or a tele-marketer. It wasn't a canvasser at the door. It wasn't a kid looking for smokes. It was an average everyday person in a jam, searching for a way out.

He was too embarrassed to be forthright. I was too blind to see that he was willing to place his trust in me. I was too busy to realize that he was asking for help. I was too busy to embrace his call for help.

The framework which I have created around me precludes helping anyone, unless I have prior plans to do so. We have built so many protections around us. We protect ourselves from the canvassers and the telemarketers. We protect ourselves from the speed traps. We protect ourselves from burglars. We protect ourselves from mind-bending advertisements. We protect ourselves from chemicals placed in food. We protect ourselves from so many who create ways to separate us from our earthly possessions.

We have learned that there are so many who choose to cheat us. With so much to think about, we have created walls that surround us. Our fears have created walls.

With all this, have we walled out part of our reality? Have we walled out the honest and caring people? Have we walled out those who desire our help? Have we walled out kindness?

How much have we walled out? We talk of kindness so trivially. It is true that we give to charities. It is true that we send money to starving children. It is true we give handouts to the beggars in the street. It is true we buy the magazines from the Jehovah's Witnesses. It is true we give to the food bank.

The question however is this: Are we truly kind, or have we forgotten how to be kind? Do we give from the heart or have we forgotten how to do this? Do we really care? Who and what do we care for? What has happened to the essence of our being? Has the world become such a miserable and dangerous place that we create a fortress around our being and hide? Do we have to do so much for ourselves that we have forgotten how to live?

It is sad to see, but it is so true because I have seen it in myself. I am grateful that my eyes have opened, even just a little. My Spirit felt shame that I did not help when I was needed. But out of my misery I find consolation in Truth, in knowing myself, in seeing who I truly am.

I have seen what I have become. I know what I can be. It only takes my courage to choose differently now.

Prayer

The Awakening

I give thanks for all that I am. I give thanks for the challenges that are before me. I give thanks for the opportunity to transcend this realm of illusions. I give thanks for the Light that shines upon me from beyond this realm, showing me the way.

I give thanks that I can choose Love and Truth to guide me. I give thanks for strength and courage to face my challenges with Love and Truth.

I give thanks for the angels who reach out to me with Love and Truth. I give thanks for the opportunities that are before me. I give thanks for the courage and strength to be a warrior of Love and Truth. I give thanks that I can see the new reality before me.

Amen.

Prayer

Prayer of Light

Call upon the Creator, the embodiment of Love and Truth, the source of enlightenment, for guidance on the journey into Light.

Call upon the Creator to awaken the Spirit of Light within, which is the essence of your being, from where all Truth and Love flows.

Give thanks for the realization that your physical body is a vessel, the house of your spiritual essence.

Seek guidance from the Creator that you may dissolve the veil between flesh and Spirit.

Seek guidance as you journey with Love and Truth, uniting your physical existence with the Light of the Spirit that shines from within.

Seek guidance that you may unite the essence of your being with the all-embracing Light shining from the Creator of life.

Amen.

Reflection

The Journey of Life

And the rains came
Like a flood it poured upon my head
And I cry as I run to seek shelter
But there is no place to hide.

The trees are without leaves
And the land is bare.
Where will I find rest?
Is it somewhere in the east?

And I walk in the rain
And there before me I see a Light
The warming soothing Light that embraces me
And touches my Spirit

Filling me with peace and Love
With the glow that is life
A new eternity before me
As I embrace that Light

And I embrace ALL that is life.
Amen.

Life offers many challenges and disappointments, but they are simply illusions of the mind. There is always hope within the realms of your Spirit, in Truth and Love. When you feel disappointment, know that you can always walk out of the rain into the warmth of the sunshine. Choose the way of the Spirit and you will always be in the warmth of the sunshine. It is the rains that brought you the wisdom to choose the path which leads onward and upward into the Light.

Meditation

Sacrifice

What are you willing to sacrifice for Truth?
What are you willing to sacrifice for Love?
What are you willing to sacrifice for joy?

What is your choice?
What path do you walk?
Do you seek the way of the Spirit?

Spirit is Truth.
Spirit is Love.
Spirit is joy.

Know who you are
For you are Spirit first
Experiencing the flesh.

Forget not who you are.
You seek balance.
Spirit in command.

Master over the flesh
It is no sacrifice.
It is being who you are.

Standing firm in your resolve
The Spirit has the will.
The flesh may waken, but Spirit has the will.

To sacrifice the flesh is no sacrifice at all, for you are Spirit first, born as Spirit and here experiencing a physical reality. As master of the flesh, Spirit shines in its brilliance in the physical world.

Reflection

Eternal Rest

Here I am
Shaken by the wind.

The cold wind blows though my bones.
And I shiver and shake
And I seek shelter from the storm.

Where is that haven with the crackling fire?
Where is that place of eternal warmth?
Where is the Truth that brings understanding?
Where is the hope that quenches my thirst?

Lead me to that fountain that will illumine me
To that Truth that I may journey into Light.

Speak to me that I may hear your voice.
Comfort my soul in times of need.

Fill my cup that I may never thirst.
Clothe me that I may never be cold.
House me that I may find eternal rest.
Amen.

The Spirit within yearns to return to that place where there is comfort and joy from oneness with life. Spirit knows its birthright and the blueprint of life. The mind has wandered far away, lost in a distant and stormy land frozen in fear. By choosing the way of the Spirit, you will find the crackling warmth that life offers within the realms of the Spirit. End your wanderings by choosing all that is Spirit and you will find that place of eternal rest.

Reflection

The Nazarene Master

Who is this Nazarene Master? It is he who walked in Nazareth in ancient times, being embraced by the power of the "I AM," the manifestation of Love and Truth. As a student of life, he embraced the totality of his being, Spirit manifesting in the flesh as one, Spirit in command of the mind and body.

His teachings were many, one of the greatest was "The Prayer to Our Father," more widely known as "The Lord's Prayer."

He was recognized as an example to be emulated, thereby acquiring the title of teacher.

He was known as Master because of his ability to command the physical and exercise control over the earth and flesh.

Reflection

The Answer

To choose in each moment
To choose in each breath
To choose from the centre of my being
To choose from my heart
To choose the desires of my Spirit

To manifest my desire
To manifest my way
To manifest my Truth
To manifest my Love

To transcend the mind
To transcend the desires of the world
To transcend the impulses of the body
To transcend the fears of survival
To transcend the controls of society

To be in each moment
To be in each breath
To be Spirit
To be Love
To be Truth
To be the one who I am

Despite the pressures of life, I am Love.
Despite the controls of society, I am Truth.
Despite the urges of the flesh, I am Spirit.
Despite the lures of the world, I am in command.
Despite the fears that grip me, I will manifest all that I am.

In command of my being, I will dwell in the secret place of my Spirit.

Reflection

Who Am I

In each moment, to have the courage.
In each breath, to have the strength.

To shine
With every thought,
Every word,
Every deed,

The Light of the Spirit
That I am.

When you know from the very depths of your being that you are Spirit first, and your life is defined by this Truth, you will see your life transformed before your very eyes.

You are Spirit. You are having a physical experience, but you have forgotten who you truly are. You have given the mind dominion. Realize that the sole responsibility of the mind is your physicality. Choose, therefore, to transcend the cycle of physical experiences, limited by the mind and the fears created therein.

You have the choice to rise above the flesh, this world and all that the mind dictates. You have the power to take command of your being, your totality. With each breath, in each moment, you can shine from the very depths of your being. Spirit is in command of the flesh, unimpeded by fear, moving in the direction that Spirit chooses, onward and upward into Light.

Illumination

Go Home

Go into that secret place of your being.

The place of Love.
The place of Truth.

The place where you manifest your desires.
The place where you are unimpeded by fears.

The place where you are in command of your being.

The place where spiritual joy is your guide.
The place where your free will is your own.

Go to that place where you can Love yourself.
Go to that place where you can honour yourself.
Go to that place where you can obey yourself.

Go to that place and live there.

Illumination

I Will Be

I will be in all my interactions all that I am.

I will be the manifestation of my word.
I will be the manifestation of Love.
I will be the manifestation of Truth.

I will be kind.
I will be accepting.
I will be creative.

I will overcome fear.
I will command the mind.
I will transcend the flesh.

I will make choices that bring joy to my being
I will be the Light that I AM.

Remember the power held within your intentions as you interact with others and create new experiences. It is the Light you are, which you shine upon those you touch, that creates life. What is your will and what do you choose to share as you manifest your will? Remember your essence, your birthright and the power you possess. Use this to manifest the life you choose. You are far more powerful than you truly realize. Spirit embraces the mind to manifest your reality, and indeed your physicality. Choose, and in so doing, create. Be mindful of your intentions and thereby direct your life, Spirit creating oneness in the flesh with the Light that you are.

Reflection

I See from My Children Who I Am

There are patterns within parents that are not yet discerned. They are the products of their environment and sojourns through time, a legacy which is manifested consciously and subconsciously, and children assume these patterns. Parents often do not even realize when they are teaching their children.

Look at the patterns of your children. There is much that disturbs you. You are looking in a mirror. Yes, it is true that they have their unique history through time, but they do need patterns to open the door to their history.

There are a multitude of opportunities here. The mirror offers the parent the opportunity to change and establish new patterns; likewise, for the children. Perhaps children will end the cycle by assuming new patterns. Such are the opportunities for mutual transformation. Such are the opportunities that are before you.

Lesson 40

The Innocence of the Children

From child to parent to child the cycle continues, and you have the will to embrace the Truth that is offered and end the cycle.

Being a parent is not an easy task regardless of the generation to which you belong. The challenges that children face today are more complex. The parents of today, however, are also more complex. In the past, your children spoke of the generation gap. You have learned that this exists regardless of generation. It is due to life's progression.

Children embrace the framework of parents, family and friends and integrate it with their own unique life force, creating a more complex state of being. If the environment is loving and kind, then children will follow that pattern. If parents smoke or drink alcohol, children will likely embrace the same pattern later in life. This happens because of subconscious, unconscious and conscious choice. When they become parents, their children do the same, and such is the cycle within which you have your existence.

When you say that you are different from your parents and they do not understand you, there is good reason. Children and parents of all generations need to realize this Truth and use it in a creative and loving way. Children are unique, just as parents are. Children, however, embrace the framework of parents and build upon it with their own, establishing a unique perspective of reality. Parents never stop learning. Children also never stop learning. Life is about expanding by experiencing. It is the way of progression whereby all Truth and reality is embraced.

The act of parenting ends at an early age of childhood. Being all that you are is a challenge not only for parents but also for all humanity. Life is about choices that bring the benefit of joy to your own state of being. Every person on this planet has this responsibility to themselves, regardless of the situation that surrounds them. When you bring joy to your own being, you are manifesting the deepest desire of the soul, and your sole purpose of existence. If you examine the basis of all religions, you will find this simple Truth.

Reflection

You Are in Command

Let not the self be controlled by the mind, otherwise the activities of the day will call to you, drawing you away to a secret place to torment you.

The mind is a tool of the Spirit but allowed to roam free will get into mischief, finding devious ways to control, using reason and fear as its favourite weapons.

Take command, for it is your free will. Command the mind to end the torment and retire into a place of quietness that the body may rest and await the command of the Spirit.

The silent mind allows you to become centred so you may meditate and allow the Spirit to find the place of oneness with the flesh.

Take command of your being and journey onward and upward into light.

Lesson 41

When You Meditate

The mind is a tool to be used by Spirit. Under the command of the Spirit, there is growth in the direction of Love and Truth. However, the mind seeks the way of the flesh, finding reasons to stray far from the way of the Spirit. Little by little, the mind is flooded and drawn away from its purpose.

When you meditate, take the time to examine the operation of your mind. Realize that mind is strong and devious and will seek to control your life in the guise of survival. You have the power to choose, to command the mind. Free will and choice are always yours.

When you meditate, embrace Spirit, command the mind and thereby set your Spirit free to direct your life.

Reflection

It Is Time To End the Cycle

Too long have you been here.
You have felt the pangs, the call.
It is time to return home.

It is time to end the cycle of birth and re-birth.
It is time to end the cycle of the flesh.
It is time to move onward into Light.

It is time to choose differently.
To make your bed in a new place.
To transcend the realm of illusion.
To move to the place that is your reality
Your true home.

Meditation

I Will

I will manifest the Light from above.
I will be the "I AM."
I will speak my Truth.

I will live upon the bread of life.
I will choose the path of Light.
I will use my power to create.

I will embrace all with Love.
Amen.

Chapter Six
Yield Not To Temptation

Introduction

In this stage of meditation, you are aware of the subtle connection between Spirit and flesh. The focus of the meditation is how it can be harnessed, the choice that determines the nature of this connection and the role passion plays.

If life is viewed as a journey in which there is suffering, you will realize that suffering offers the opportunity to choose differently. Through meditation you become aware of this opportunity and the choices that are offered. You already have the power to choose differently and walk along a new path.

On this path, you will grow and change, for it is a journey of healing transformation. The power of healing restores the building blocks of your life so the Light of the Spirit may shine through the flesh. True healing comes from manifesting the desires of Spirit through the flesh.

The flesh is a manifestation of Spirit. In other words, you are Spirit seeking expression, reaching into the physical realm through the flesh. You are Spirit first, simply wearing a clothing of flesh. The dichotomy between Spirit and flesh emerges when the mind imposes its power through the physical body. The mind will exercise this power based on its perception of life. Left unguided, the mind will operate solely upon the premise of survivability, seeking to protect you from physical harm and will also make valiant efforts to maintain control of your complete life.

The way of the mind is a legacy, which you can choose to transcend. As Spirit, you have the power to command the totality of your being if you so choose. You can command the mind. The freedom to choose is your true power. Embrace this power and you can walk the enlightened path.

Enlightenment is a state of being in which you are in command of your mind. The passion of Spirit is to shine its Light through the flesh. By commanding the mind to manifest the guidance that Spirit offers, you end the dichotomy between Spirit and flesh. Suffering will cease and true joy will emerge out of this unity, and you will become aware of your true purpose here on Earth.

The Orange Glow

When you feel the desire to create or have expression, the energy of the second chakra is present. When this area is activated, it is passion that emerges and fills your being. It can happen any time. You feel an urge within. Whether it is in the form of your sexual biology or the desire to create something material, it is all from one source. It manifests in different ways.

You can feel your passion during meditation by placing your focus on the second chakra. The energy which emerges vibrates at the frequency of the colour orange.

A life that is filled with passion is one that is also filled with joy. It is a joy that is felt to the depths of the Spirit. Joy is much like a barometer which reflects your spiritual state of being. You find joy when you walk the road, which you have entered this realm to travel. You find joy when you manifest the desires of the Spirit. You find joy when there is balance between flesh and Spirit. When you are filled with joy, you shine with brilliance.

Passion is the expression of your Spirit and is manifested in many ways. For example, Spirit is aware of the fundamental need to nourish the physicality. If the body is lacking a particular nutrient, an inner need, desire or passion for food with that nutrient surfaces.

The expression of sexual biology, which is a channel of release for creative energy, is another example. The mind plays with this; thus, this area of your being is called the sex chakra. Consequently, society largely equates passion with the biology of sex.

Open your eyes and you will see that time is repeating and you have before you an opportunity to gather the lessons from the past and end this cycle.

Know the Truth of this energy when you feel it within your being and the manner of expression that you will choose. Will it be flesh or Spirit?

The energy within your body is always in a dance, flowing up and down. As it rises from the base chakra, it makes its way to the third, then spills onto the second chakra, which is located above the sexual glands. You can feel it within you as a potent and powerful source of energy.

In this meditation, contemplate the relationship between Spirit and flesh and how the energy from this chakra seeks expression through passion. You can <u>feel</u> this passion. You can feel the desire to manifest Spirit, here in the flesh, by stilling the mind and allowing your life essence to emerge.

You can feel the passion to create. You can feel the passion rising out of your sexuality. You can feel the burning desire [passion] to express this from the depths of your physicality. For example, the artist feels the desire to paint.

In meditation, you will be guided to manifest this passion as a function of your free will. Misguided, how will this passion seek expression? Spirit is always the ever-present guide. You have the free will to accept this guidance and command the flesh. You have the free will to express your passion in any way you choose. It is always your choice. The barometer of spiritual joy rises when you choose to manifest the passion of Spirit through your physicality.

Choice determines how this energy will be utilized. The power of your will, which emerges from the third chakra, directs how this energy is manifested. Will you use it for the gratification of your sexuality and physical appetites, or will you use it for the manifestation of spiritual Love through creative expression? Will you use it to unite Spirit and cells in the expression of Love for the creation of life? Realize that the expression of Love and Truth is passion; likewise, passion of the Spirit is an expression of Love and Truth.

Your expression, whether by word, thought or deed, is a function of the energy which emanates from the area of this chakra. You have the power to choose and thereby navigate your path. Choose to command the mind to manifest the desire of the Spirit. Realize that the mind can be used as a tool of the Spirit to manifest desire though choice. Will you choose the way of the flesh or the way of the Spirit? What is the way of the Spirit? It is always the expression of Love. The way of the Spirit is the desire to create. It is the path of eternal joy. The way of the flesh is the path of unconscionable survival of self. The way of the self is one of self-gratification and self-aggrandizement.

Let your attitude always be one of Love and acceptance. Know that you will be challenged. Each challenge is an opportunity to transcend the way of the flesh, choose the way of Spirit and manifest your power to choose Love and Truth.

You will also be challenged by energies that exist in other realms, relentlessly seeking expression through your first and second chakras. When these areas become active, be aware of the source of the energy. Explore your attitudes to determine if they are founded upon Spiritual Love and Truth or from another source.

Love is the energy of the Spirit. Love transcends science, reason and physicality. What is the foundation of your attitudes? Are they founded upon the desires of your own Spirit? Let your life be a living example of Love. Acceptance without condition, expectation or judgment is an offer of your physicality as a living sacrifice, that others may have the opportunity to gain the lessons of Love. In so doing, the power of Love expands from your fourth chakra through the second to embrace humanity with the trans-forming and healing energies of the Spirit.

When you express your creativity with the passion of the Spirit by choosing the way of Love, energy will flow from your heart area, reaching the second chakra and tempering your attitudes. When faced with difficult situations, remember that you always have a choice. Will your choice emanate a pure brilliant orange by being creative in all your actions, deeds and words? Will you use the tempering energy of Love flowing from the fourth chakra, embracing your power to overcome the temptation to gratify the flesh?

When you choose the path of creativity, utilizing the passion of your Spirit, your journey will be filled with the pure, clear Light of life. The energy which emanates from the area of the second chakra will grow, seen within your aura as a glow of brilliant orange.

New Life

A "miracle" is the result of the passion of the Spirit. The miracle of life here in this realm is the function of the passion of the Spirit. Birth is a miracle of life resulting from the unity of energies, the sole purpose of which is the opportunity for growth into Light. The environment needed for growth is unique. The energies that create the drama needed for growth are also unique.

Imagine what is required to produce a successful Broadway play. Actors and actresses together with a multitude of extras with certain characteristics and talents all set the stage. It is the same with growth and transformation. Actors and actresses are needed. The environment is needed. A certain level of morality is needed. The political environment, social norms and religious practices all play a part in setting the stage. However, you are not acting. It is your life that is unfolding before your very eyes. It is personal choice that sets the stage and direction of the play.

The timeline of life is a moving stage that has been set by spiritual cooperation. You have chosen to be here at this point in the timeline. You have chosen your parents, brothers, sisters, friends and the environment within which you exist. The stage is set. However, life is not governed solely by such pre-defined fate. There is freedom of choice. The environment has been created by free will, but the freedom to choose remains, and can change the environment and your path, and the path of all involved, anytime. Fate is simply your own plan of pre-destiny to face your own self, and experience what you choose, with whom you choose, which you can change at any time.

Spirit from within directs life, if you accept what is offered. Your Spirit is intrinsically aware of the path you have chosen. It is this guidance that takes you along the path of transformation. It is this guidance that manifests the environment for your undoing.

When you embrace Love, which flows from the fourth chakra, it takes you on this path of transformation. You radiate Love, offering the hand of transformation to all who participate in the drama of life. It opens the door for the manifestation of energies through the first chakra, inviting new life into this realm to complete the stage. Spirit and cells unite in a dance of creativity.

Always be true to yourself by choosing the pathway of Love. It will lead you to self-fulfillment. It will open the doorway of transformation, for self and those who require your cooperation by participating in the stage of life. It navigates your journey onward and upward into the pure, clear and bright Light of your life.

Second Chakra Meditation

The purpose of this meditation is to harmonize body, mind and Spirit to expand the energy from the area of the second chakra. The aura this energy radiates is as a brilliant orange which flows down from the sixth to the fourth then the second chakra.

As you meditate, focus on the area of the second chakra, located in the middle of the abdomen. The symbol to keep in mind is "temptation." You will feel the temptation to follow old patterns. The flesh will tempt you. You will be tempted by energies that seek to idolize your physicality. Attitudes from the past will seek expression. Your Spirit, mind and body will seek expression.

This chakra corresponds with cells located in the pancreas, responsible for the generation of certain hormones which stimulate the pituitary. This area becomes active during puberty. In meditation, focus a few inches below the solar plexus.

Why temptation? This is the area of expression that is borne out of desire. You can choose the manner of expression. You can choose to manifest second chakra energies for the gratification of physical appetites, or you may choose to manifest these energies in a creative manner, in accordance with the desires of your Spirit and the path of spiritual Love.

You can feel the passion to create as it rises out of this area of your being. The first chakra is the source and bread of life. It is this area where Spirit and cells unite in the dance of creation (chapter four). Both energy centres work in harmony with each other in the expression of your life. How will you express your passion? Will you grow flowers or thorns?

As you meditate, receive the guidance, strength and courage to transcend the temptation to satisfy the yearnings of the flesh and the material world. Choose the Spirit within to be your ever-present counsellor and guide. Let your works always be a function of the

Love of your Spirit and transcend the boundaries of fear, created by the mind.

When spiritual Love governs your choice, you glow with happiness. Shining from the area of the second chakra is the energy of creativity, which fills your aura with a brilliant orange.

Preparation

Meditation requires preparation. It is a sacred act and you are a sacred being. Your needs are unique. Deep within there is a sacred knowingness, the foundation of meditation, where you become aware of your needs. As you look within and explore your needs, honour all parts of your being, body, mind and Spirit.

To prepare for this meditative journey, first you must find your spiritual centre, the place of your knowingness. As you seek this place, your Spirit will fill your consciousness with awareness, which is the Truth and will guide you. Have the faith that Spirit will be your guide. Have the faith that you will find the place of your knowingness. Go into meditation with the expectation that your spiritual needs will be fulfilled and your body and mind will be guided by Spirit.

Prepare to journey to a place within, where you are Light, Truth and Love.

Feel the desire to still your mind as you prepare to leave the busy world that surrounds you.

Gentle exercise helps with relaxation. Before you meditate, go for a walk, practice yoga or take a good stretch. All these will help to align and open channels for the flow of energy within.

Breathing exercises bring balance. As you prepare to go into meditation, take three deep and gentle breaths. Let these be comfortable and controlled breaths. As you inhale, fill your being with energy. Feel the energy enter your lungs. Hold your breath for a comfortable period of time, then allow the breath to rush from your body. As it does, allow yourself to relax. With each breath become more and more relaxed.

After these three breaths, take time to pray. Seek the presence of the Creator of life. Seek the presence of your guides and teachers who offer Love and Truth. Seek the Love and protection of the angels. As you prepare for meditation, feel your desires and aspirations flow from your very own heart.

Prayer

Divine Creator, I ask for your presence at this time of humble meditation. Fill me with Light from the crown of my head to the soles of my feet, permeating each cell within my body that I may feel and know your presence. I ask for the presence of my guides to embrace me with the oneness of eternal Love and Truth. I ask for the angels to come forth and stand beside me with sacred council, behind me for protection and in front of me to show the way. For all these blessings, I am truly thankful. Amen.

Healing Waters- Guided Imagery

As you relax, you are cradled within the arms of the angels. Feel the energy that surrounds you. Feel the energy that is radiating from the Light that is shining upon you. Feel the energy of the angels who embrace you. Feel the energy of the earth beneath your feet. Feel the oneness of life and Light.

In the stillness of your physical body, feel the power of your Spirit. Realize that you are Spirit first and in Spirit, all things are possible.

Your body is a temple of your Spirit and has the freedom to leave if you so choose. In your stillness, prepare for a journey of the Spirit. Visualize your Spirit leaving your physicality, ready to explore the reality beyond. Visualize a crystal stairway with seven steps.

Place one foot upon the first step as you transcend this realm, shedding the weight of your physicality. With each step, one at a time, make your way to the top where you will find a door. Open this door and behold a new reality. Enter these gates with thankfulness and expectancy, for before you is the totality of your life.

The angels greet you. In this place, you feel free to embrace all the wonders and beauty of reality. Here you experience nature in its pristine, pure and untouched form. Your entire being tingles as you feel a golden presence that fills the place with a warm and loving Light. Feel the embrace of this Light shining around you.

Take a walk through this wonderful place. Follow the flower-lined pathway to the trees beyond where you will find rivers of pure water flowing from the fountain of Truth. As you look within the trees, fed by the peaceful rivers, there is a pool of silvery water. The gentle breeze brings calm to your entire being. Flowers of every colour dance around the water. The birds sing a melodious tune and the butterflies flutter about, filling the air with magic.

You feel drawn to enter the water. The angels go before you and beckon you to follow. You feel calm and protected in their presence. Leaving your clothes behind, you follow the angels into the water. The temperature is perfect, not too cold and not too warm. You feel buoyant. You feel like a baby with the protection of loving hands nearby. You are free of fear in the safety of the angels who bear you up upon the water as you float about in delight.

With the touch of the water, you can feel its transforming power. You can feel its life-giving energy as it bathes your body.

Feel the healing energy of the waters soothe you. Feel the embrace of Love and Truth, which bathes you, and all that does not serve Spirit fades into the water. Feel your entire being glisten with the Light from within. Feel the purity of your Spirit. Feel all that you are. Feel the Light from within permeate your body, each cell, as the healing waters cleanse you.

Your teachers join you in the water. Their presence fills you with joy. You feel their Love. You feel the embrace of Truth to the depths of your being. You feel the oneness with Truth.

Take all the time that you need in this place as you receive the Truth offered by your teachers. Take the time to communicate with the angels, to receive the embrace of their Love. Take the time to receive the healing energy of the water and feel the transforming energy of the Creator's Light which fills this place of such joy.

[Pause]

Second Chakra

As you embrace the transforming energy of the waters, take the time to focus on your entire being, on every chakra, starting from the crown, one at a time. As you focus on the second chakra, the area of creativity, receive of the strengthening and purifying energy flowing from the healing waters. Feel the desire to transcend the flesh. Feel the desires of your Spirit to still the mind and the body, to Love, manifest Truth and embrace the blissful state of spiritual awareness. Your angels and teachers guide you. Become empowered. Realize that you have the power to transform ideas and feelings into substance. Take the time to explore the source of this power, and how you will utilize it. Consult with your angels and teachers. Consult with your Creator of life. Pray for guidance.

Prayer

I ask the angels who walk with me to protect, guide and council me. I ask my teachers who walk with me to share Truth that will unlock the door to my Spirit. I pray for the blessings of the Light which surrounds me that I will be guided by Love and Truth, now and always. Amen.

[Pause]

Seek within. Know your intentions. Does your Spirit from within direct your intentions? Are your intentions borne out of the desire to be creative? Are your intentions fuelled by Love?

You have the free will to choose in all things, always. Choice is the directing force. Choice is your power. You can choose the way of the Spirit, which is Love and Truth. In this sacred place of healing waters, gather the strength and courage to choose the way of the Spirit, where its ideals and virtues become the ideas and attitudes you manifest in the flesh.

Know yourself. Know Spirit. Know what is of the flesh. Remember that your second chakra is the area of passion. It is the area of desire. Your physical body responds to stimuli from the physical, mental and spiritual. Remember that the mind focuses on the survivability of the flesh. Your mind embraces the senses to become aware of its physicality.

What is the directing force of the mind? Is the mind fuelled by fear based on the survival of the flesh? By the need for abundance? The desire to experience the sensations of the flesh? The desire to aggrandize the flesh?

Here in these healing waters, embrace the Truth of who you are. Embrace Spirit. Spirit is passion. Spirit is desire. Spirit is Love.

The mind is a channel of your passion, your desire. Know what is an illusion and what is real. Recognize that your choices can bring either joy or pain, and the joys of the flesh fade with the flesh.

Spirit is the desire to create with Love and Truth. The power to choose comes from Spirit. It is your power. Realize that the Spirit can choose to command the mind. The Spirit can choose how to channel the power of the second chakra, passion, and be guided by Love. Spirit can choose Truth as the fabric of all that emerges from the second chakra.

Will you choose the way of the Spirit and use your passion to plant seeds of Love and Truth, which will blossom into Light?

Passion
The purity of life is the passion of the Spirit. Choose to manifest Love and Truth with passion. As this energy, this passion emerges from within; choose Spirit to be your guide, channel your passion, create with Love and Truth. When you feel the urge from within to express your energy, choose to create with Love and Truth. Let your life, your days, your minutes, your moments be filled with passion, directed and re-directed by Spirit. Let your mantra be passion, creativity, Love and Truth.

Your angels and teachers will always be at your side, guiding you, if you so choose. Seek this guidance. Seek their embrace in the healing waters, and pray that they will be with you when you need them as you journey onward in the physical realm.

[Pause]

It is now time to leave the healing waters and return to the physical realm. Give thanks for the healing that you received.

Accept the blessings of Love from the angels. Accept the blessings of Truth from your teachers. Accept the blessings of healing from the Creator of life.

Accept the embrace of your teachers. Accept the embrace of your guides. Accept the embrace of your Creator of life.

Although you may feel that you do not wish to return, you need to continue your work in the physical realm, to journey onward and upward. You may choose to return, armed with all you have received.

It is time to return and embrace the consciousness of your physicality. Feel the beat of your heart and the life-giving energy rushing through your veins, from the crown of your head to the tips of your toes. As your consciousness returns to embrace your physicality, feel the sensation of your body. You may gently open your eyes, adjusting to the Light and Love of the physical realm that surrounds you.

Once again, give thanks for all that you have received. Ask for guidance here in the physical realm that you may embrace the Light of Love and Truth and be filled with joy as you continue on your journey onward and upward into the Light of life.

Prayer
Divine Creator, I give thanks for your Light and pray for the courage and strength to embrace the passion of Spirit, and manifest Love and Truth in all my actions, on my journey onward and upward, embraced by your Light. Amen.

Lesson 42

The Power to Create

Breathe.
Feel it.
You are power.
Within, you will find the greatest power.

Realize that tomorrow is within the grasp of your heart. Yes, it is true that tomorrow will never come, and life is in this very moment; however, it is your imagination that will define your reality, imagination of what tomorrow can be. Therefore, imagine your tomorrow and create it now, in this very moment. It is all within your grasp. You have the power to manifest, to be all that you choose. It lies within your reach, within your second chakra.

Breathe and feel the power within. With each breath, grow strong, choose and manifest all that you are. You are the creator of your being. Know that it is the choices of today that manifest the blueprint of your tomorrow. Choose and become all that you can imagine. Become all that you are, the image of Love and Truth, in this very moment. Amen.

Lesson 43

New Life

As you journey
The life before you
Is the opportunity
Which offers mighty challenges.

It is the voice of the Spirit which calls
Beckoning you on
Pointing the way.

Offering a new song
A sweet melody.

And the heart sings
As new life is born.

Reflection

Build Your House Upon a Rock

The realms beyond are vast. It is there that you will have your existence when you move on and bid farewell to your physicality. Your home will become what you have created, the framework of your being-ness.

What are your aspirations within this consciousness you call your physicality? What do you create? Your physicality is only an illusion, and all that you create within this illusion will fall away as you move on. Then, what will remain?

Have you forged bonds of Love? Have you built relationships founded upon Truth? Have you purged your being with fire so you are fully cleansed?

When your physicality disappears, what will remain? Fear not, for what is built by Spirit will remain for eternity. Build treasures in a place where you will choose to remain for eternity.

As you have your being, consider the purpose and meaning of freedom from the illusion of this realm. Consider this whenever you choose.

Amen.

Reflection

Creating and Manifesting Your Reality

In your going out and coming in, Truth is revealed. It is the journey along the pathway of life. Your awareness of nature and the physical realm grows. You learn how to transcend the physical and channel Love and Truth from the realms beyond. You learn how to embrace all that you are. You learn how to manifest the desire of the Spirit within.

On this journey, you transcend physical existence and unite with the Light that shines from the centre of your being. Your consciousness embraces the true reality of existence. You realize all that you have accepted as real is not, and what you have assumed is not, in Truth will last for all of eternity. You learn that your thoughts exist in a reality beyond the perception of the physical senses, and through meditation you can embrace the fullness of your physicality and travel beyond it.

What does life in this realm offer and what does life in the realms beyond offer? What is the purpose of each level of existence and how do you embrace the opportunities of each? The answer lies within, in a place where Spirit offers bliss. It is the desire of Spirit to manifest bliss in your physical experience.

The first step is to gain an understanding of this realm. On the journey of life, you become aware of false happiness, which disappears as soon as the money is spent, the car gets rusty or the house loses its newness and charm. You also understand that there is happiness which cannot be touched by the elements of nature, the trials of time or a diminishing bank account. As you travel the road of life and grow, it becomes clear that your goal is to find the source of eternal happiness, and embrace it. You become aware that this is the desire of your Spirit that dwells within.

As you grow and embrace the power of your thoughts, you learn how to create whatever you choose. You learn of the power of the mind, and how to apply the sense of meditation. You learn how to embrace all that exists in this realm. You learn how to access the realm beyond and establish a reality that is eternal, a place where you can go whenever you choose, one that will exist when you transcend this realm and walk to the other side of the door of physical life.

You are the Ashram that you create. Your Truth is the building block. Your Love creates its form. The life you build in a secret place in the realms beyond, out of the finer fabrics of life, is that part of you that will survive beyond the physical and exist for eternity. This place is your sanctuary, a place of strength and spiritual sustenance. Whenever you choose, retire into this secret place of the Spirit for sustenance and comfort.

In this place, you will find the schools of higher learning, which will offer needed lessons. You may learn how to construct your house or mansion or temple, indeed your Ashram. It is the place where you will meet with your guides, teachers and loved ones. It is all within your grasp. It is the essence of your true being.

In the physical realm, as you perform tasks that meet the needs of your physicality, let your choices reflect the aspirations of Spirit, sustaining both the physical and spiritual in balance, thereby embracing all that is eternal. It is your choice. You can, if you choose, manifest the eternal and fill your being with joy that does not fade with the noonday sun. Choose, therefore, Love and Truth, the building blocks of your life, on the journey onward and upward. Amen.

Lesson 44

Energy

This lesson is about energy and transformation. It is about who you are, now and in the beginning. What purpose does each form of energy have in this realm, and in all realms?

There are lessons all around us, each day, each moment and with each breath. Have you taken the time to look at nature such as the birds of the field? It is truly a marvel to observe. There are so many different species, and you can see how they bring balance. Some eat from the soil; others, the flowers. Each plays an individual role in the cycle of life. Their unique power brings balance in this realm.

As you look closer, you see that there are energies that convert waste matter to soil so that it can be used by another form of life, For example, trees that bring forth fruit, which take from the fertile soil. Then the life-giving energy of the sun plays its part in the grand cycle of life. What happens to life and balance when these energies change?

In the beginning, there was Eden, and all were in balance. Man then appeared in the picture and sought experience, changing the balance. Today you can see the delicate balance still changing, each moment, and in different ways. You see inhumanity within our county and between countries. Pollution fills the air, water and earth. Animals and plants become extinct. The earth groans as the soil is covered with concrete and asphalt. Why? Is it because of something positive or greed? Is it because of Love or the fear of lack?

Is the world perfect? Seek within and you will find the answer.

What does your mind allow you to see? Is the Truth hidden from your view? Is your perception of reality clouded? There are so many different aspects of existence that cloud the perception of reality, such as wants, desires and apathy.

Is it Truth that you can feel hurt? It does not make you any less than perfect when you feel pain. Does it alter your perception of Truth? The ancient teachers have offered the Truth that you are energy, living Light wearing clothing made of the flesh.

If you are living Light, then why do you feel pain?

All of existence harmonizes like an orchestra playing melodious music. When you look at the energy of all the forces of nature in balance here in this realm, you can see and feel the beauty and harmony. It is truly a wonder to see the cherry blossoms, the bees, the birds feeding, the sun shining, the rain, the wind, the sky and the clouds all in a rhythmic dance. Such is the wonderful music of this realm.

Energy in motion is the dance of life. But like an orchestra, when one is out of tune, it affects the whole. When you feel pain and discord, the angels weep, and the hurt they feel is far greater than you can ever imagine, for such is the way of the Love that embraces all.

All plays a part in existence. Perfect in every way, you strive to fully manifest the Light, which is your Spirit. You strive to walk back to that place from where you came. You are born of the Light, and once again you journey, seeking your true nature, to be fully embraced by the Light. Your Spirit yearns for this embrace and feels the pain of this yearning. The angels reach out with open arms to receive, and welcome you once more to a place where you can be all that you are.

Energy in motion is the opportunity for transformation. Here you are in this place, this moment, this breath. The music has started. You are on the road of transformation. What do you need for the journey back to the Light, where you dance to the rhythm of life?

You simply need to be all that you are and nothing more.

Reach within and grasp your power, the energy that emerges from within. Be guided by this Light of the Spirit. Embrace and walk as Spirit clothed in flesh, one day to yield the clothing and return to your fullness, from where you journeyed.

The yearnings of the Spirit are deep and here to be satisfied: To be all that you are, transformed, Spirit and flesh as one, a being of living Light, to dance with the angels and walk in eternal bliss.

Thanks to Creator of life for this blessing.

Amen.

Lesson 45

Faith

You can say to the sea, gather up your fish into the waves and cast them upon the shore that I may take and eat, and the sea will obey your very word, if you have such faith.

Who are you? Are you Spirit or flesh? What is the power you hold within your bosom that your word may command the sea?

Faith comes from the embrace of your totality. It is within your knowingness that such power emerges and you can command the sea to cast its fish upon the shore. It is your word which commands such power, for you are your word and your word is the manifestation of your Spirit.

You can manifest your power through thought, the raw material, and imagination, the blueprint of your intention. Your word is an extension of yourself, which carries your commands and power. The universe is the builder that manifests your will. All that this requires is faith, the engine which drives the process of manifestation.

You are all that you are and the creator of your totality. Faith is the power to embrace what your mind cannot see or accept. Is faith part of your totality? Where do you find such faith? Is it in this chapter of your life? It is if you so choose.

Lesson 46

Wisdom

"Wisdom comes with age." You have heard this so many times. Is there some Truth to the statement? Wisdom comes with experience. You can shout Truth from the rooftops, but they are only empty words until they take form when your personal experience speaks them.

It is Truth that life is about the facing of self. This is wisdom that can only be realized with experience.

You can spend your entire life seeking what you think will bring happiness, only to recognize that you seek a false promise. The promise of true happiness comes from facing self. It does not matter if you are rich or poor, strong or weak, sick or healthy. Happiness is not found in these material states. The journey of seeking these brings wisdom. On this journey, you learn that the happiness found on the material path is false and empty, dissolving quickly. Eternal happiness comes from uncovering the Light you hold within and shining this Light, despite the material conditions that exist around you.

Is it wise to seek happiness that does not fade with the noonday sun, or a bank account? You are already wise. Seek within and you will know the Truth.

Lesson 47

Family

You invite your children to this physical world with an agreement that you will offer a framework within which they will have opportunities to become all that they are. The converse is also true. Children join you in this realm so they can offer opportunities for parents to become all that they are. It is a symbiotic relationship. Once this is realized, you can approach this relationship so you embark on a journey of creative sharing. It is a journey upon which there is mutual acceptance without condition, expectation or judgment.

Reflection

Is It True?

What part of my being creates choice?
Is it the body?
Is it the mind?
Is it the emotional self?
Is it the Spirit that is manifested in the physical?
Is it the Spirit that is a spark of God?
Is it the oneness with life?

Am I an extension of God?
Is life based upon choice?

Is it true that all I am is a result of my choices?
Is it true that the perimeter of my being is defined by my fears?
Is it true that fear is an illusion?
Is it true that my choice will take me beyond the limits established
by fear?
Is it true that I expand when I go beyond my fears?
Is it true that I can expand my being to embrace all of existence by
simply choosing?
Is it true that I have the freedom to choose, and it cannot be taken
away, unless I choose to give it away?

Why do I fear to choose?
Is it a choice that I have made?
Is it true that I can choose differently?
Is it true that I can choose to embrace the Light?
Is it true that I am the Light?
Amen.

Meditation

I Feel

I feel heaven that I seek.
I feel Spirit that I am.
I feel Truth that is and shall be.
I feel the life I manifest.
I feel the patterns of the past.
I feel the desire to create.
I feel Love to transform my life.
Amen.

Illumination

Feelings

I long for the moment when my being will know the feeling of oneness with the flesh as Spirit emerges to command, rise above, sing a new song, shine with joy.

To know the feeling of heaven
To see the shimmering images of Spirit
To feel the eyes of Spirit open
To feel the gentle touch of Spirit
To feel the power and embrace of Truth
To feel Spirit manifest free will
To feel abundance as seen by Spirit
To feel the power of silencing the mind
To feel Spirit choose a new path
To feel Spirit create new life
To feel Spirit express Love
To feel the power to transform with Love
To feel the emergence of the I AM.

Chapter Seven

Love and Deliverance

Introduction

What is the greatest form of Love? Love is the essence of life and like blood, it is a vehicle which feeds your Spirit. When there is a state of balance within your being, Love flows from the seventh chakra down to the fourth. It is the connection you hold with the Creator of all of life. As this connection with life expands and flows, spilling over, the Love continues to flow, now from the fourth chakra to the third, tempering the will, your power, and injecting it with Love. Love spills from the fourth to the second, embracing your creativity. Love flows from the fourth to the first, dissolving fear. When you meditate, you seek a state of balance to open the channels within you for the flow of energy. You are opening the channels of your own life force which lay dormant.

You are the directing force of your life. You have the power to command the flow of this energy within your being. You have the power to command the flow between the chakras and radiate Love. You have the power to inject Love in all your interactions. As you meditate, remember that this energy is your life force. It is who you are and you have the power to make it become the directing force in your life.

Balance comes from harmony among the chakras and this is achieved with meditation. The fourth chakra acts as a bridge between the upper and lower chakras. Look upon the upper three as the patterns. When there is balance, the patterns from above (the upper three) flow freely to the lower three, as the fourth chakra, the bridge, injects the tempering energy of Love. Such balance is the source of abundant Love, which satisfies the needs of the etheric body and further spills over into all the activities of your life, tempering your intentions with the power of Love.

In this way, the activities of the first three chakras are transformed by the energy from the fourth. Fourth chakra energy heals and gives life. It is an energy that manifests absolute acceptance. It is an energy that is free from all conditions, expectations and judgment. As this state of balance is achieved, this energy becomes visible in your aura and seen with the eyes of the Spirit as a brilliant green glow.

Sparkling with Green

Let every day be a green day. Let every moment be a green moment. What does this mean? Use the energy that emanates from the area of the heart to be your deliverer in every situation. Like fire upon steel, choose to temper all your actions, thoughts, words and deeds with Love. When you are faced with any challenge, have no fear. Simply apply the energy which radiates from the fourth chakra, the centre of your being. As you respond, add the dimension of Love, for it is the power you hold within and delivered with choice. Then let your expectations be fuelled with hope, anticipating an outcome embraced by joy. With Love, you have the power to transform life, your own life, and in so doing, to touch others, perhaps planting seeds of hope within them.

For example, it is easy to become angry with a slow clerk at a grocery store checkout. How do you manifest frustration or anger? Should you exercise your power to choose differently? You can search for the opportunities being offered in this unique situation. Realize that all situations offer lessons and remember you always have the choice to manifest your power which flows from the fourth chakra. You can choose to radiate Love, as it is acceptance without condition or expectation. Love is free from all forms of judgment. Choose always to maintain and radiate a state of Love.

How can you manifest this Love? Respond with Love. Choose to be accepting of someone who may be inexperienced, tired or frustrated with belligerent customers, or perhaps have a difficult personal life. Perhaps it is a teenager who just found out that she is pregnant. Perhaps it's a husband who just learned that his wife has cancer.

Become an example of Love. Choose another lane. Bless the clerk with the energy radiating from your heart, with kind words and a gentle smile. Become an example of Love and pray that others will follow your example as you exercise patience, acceptance and kindness. Pray that you can always be a living example of Love.

Who Are You?

The questions remain: Who is God and who is the Creator? Who are you and what is Spirit? What is a soul? These are questions about the understanding of your own self.

There are many different answers to these questions, for the mind is an amazing tool that creates concepts and perceptions for your satisfaction. The Spirit, however, continues to seek until an appropriate answer is found. Satisfaction comes only when there is a knowingness. Such knowingness is your connection with Truth.

Truth is who you are. As has been given, it is the foundation and building blocks of who you are. It is the yarn in the fabric of your being. Truth is what is and will always be. You are a spark of the Light that is life; thus, you are one and the same as the source, and seen a child of the Light. What is the Light? It is the energy of your life. It is what you are. You are a being of Light. God and the Creator is one and the same. God and the Creator is Light, of which you are a part. You were born of Light. Your Spirit and Light are unique and individual and separate, yet one and the same, as a father and son is the same.

Why are you here and what is your purpose? Choice brought you here. You were curious and you seek experience. It was your nature and still is. You journeyed on one experience after another, creating your consciousness. With a changing consciousness, you went deeper into this physical reality, until you forgot who you truly are and identified only with the consciousness you are aware of now. You now see yourself with the eyes of flesh. This consciousness can be viewed as your soul. Within, however, you have an awareness of the Truth. You have an awareness of who you truly are. This is the part of you that yearns to embrace all that you are and continually nags you to find answers. This part of you knows your true nature and desperately seeks to return. This is your Spirit. The part of you that identifies with the consciousness you are aware of is your mind. The mind is fed by the physical senses, which defines its awareness. The nature and mandate of the mind is protection and self-preservation, which it does very well. If you are in danger, the mind reacts immediately and you run or fight. The adrenaline starts flowing immediately so you can take yourself out of danger. This is one true purpose of the mind, mandated by your Spirit.

There is always a battle between the mind and Spirit. The mind embraces the mandate of the Spirit for protection but also seeks control in the process. It loves the familiar and tries to keep you there. If you try to venture beyond, it creates fear and uses logic to convince you to remain. Items such as fear, reason, procrastination or science are the weapons used against your Spirit. Thus, you will see that the mind has become the tool of stagnation. Your true purpose is realized by commanding the mind. Yes, you have continued to allow the mind to play, now and through eternity, to explore its curiosity and experience different aspects of reality. Since you have become lost in this reality and your Spirit seeks to return, it is incumbent upon you to navigate a path back to your true reality, expanding your consciousness to embrace all once again. This is done by choice. You Spirit can command your mind to pave the pathway back to your source. It is simple. Just choose it, and command your mind to do it.

Give your mind a task. It will work on it and amaze you. Your mind is amazing. Your body is amazing. Your Spirit is amazing. All of you is simply amazing. Realize that you are amazing and embrace your brilliance to manifest all that you are.

The nature of your Spirit is threefold. It is Truth. Love is like the glue that binds the building blocks of Truth. It guides the yarn in the fabric of who you are. The nature of your Spirit is happiness. When you choose happiness, you are travelling on a path back to your source. When you choose happiness, you are choosing who you are.

Your Mystical Nature

Three above and three below are the numbers. The pattern is above. Choose to manifest this pattern in your physical life, "As above so below." Manifest the will of the Spirit here on Earth as in the words that were given. "Thy will be done on earth, as it is in heaven."

Look closely and you will see your numbers, three above thrice and three below thrice. Know the meaning of the number and you will escape judgment by embracing your truth with Love and joy.

You have a secret name, one given to you at birth, when you were born into Light. Seek within and you will know this name. It is a name that represents who you are. Take the time to be committed to yourself, seek this name and share it with no one. Allow the power held in your name to infuse within you the essence of who you are. Remember that you are Light, born of Light. Shine in your brilliance as this power infuses into your being.

Who are you? Let your own Spirit answer as you open the door which leads to the very depths of your being, out of which will flow the essence of who you are: Love, Truth and Joy.

Fourth Chakra Meditation

The purpose of this meditation is to harmonize body, mind and Spirit so the energy from the area of the fourth chakra expands to emanate a pure and brilliant green glow.

As you meditate, focus on the area of this chakra, which corresponds with the thymus sitting behind the heart in the chest cavity. According to medical journals, this gland is responsible for immunity from disease. Much like the white blood cells which fend off diseases within the physical body, the energy from this area can temper the activities of the lower three chakras, bringing harmony and balance to your being.

The fourth chakra is well-known as the area where Love is manifested. Thus, as you face the challenge of balancing the lower three chakras, incorporate the energy of the fourth, which is Love. When faced with the slow clerk at the checkout, resist the instinctive tendency to react with anger which can emerge from the area of the third chakra. Instead, choose to embrace the transforming and tempering power of Love which flows from your heart area and can inject understanding and acceptance into the situation with a smile or a few kind words. Let Love be your "deliverer from evil." Realize that patterns such as reacting with anger, which do not serve your Spirit, can be viewed as "evil."

The symbol to keep in mind during this meditation is the transforming power of "Love." When there is balance, this area fills your aura with a brilliant green glow.

Prayer

Divine Creator, I ask that the words of my mouth and meditations of my heart bestow healing to my mind, body and Spirit. I ask for the gift of protection that you may surround me with your Light during this time of meditation, and that I may be guided by your

Love and Truth to manifest joy in my life. Amen.

Doorway of the Heart
As you enter meditation, please be prepared to receive of the Light that shines from the realms beyond, which you will feel in the area of the heart.

During the meditation feel free to pause to allow the Light to penetrate your being with its transforming energy. Be prepared to be touched by the gentle kisses of Light that flow from above to embrace your entire being.

Sit comfortably with your back gently erect and feet flat on the floor. Have your hands loosely placed on your lap, palms facing down, or if you are so guided, you may choose palms facing up with the thumb and index finger forming a circle, symbolizing the completion in life. Do whatever makes you feel comfortable and connected so you may go into a deep meditation. What is important during meditation is your feeling of comfort and relaxation.

As you relax, you are preparing yourself to enter the realm of the Creator. As you relax, you physically prepare your body and your mind for this meeting.

Breathe in and out, with continuous breaths, gently and slowly, and allow all the comfort and peace that you can gather to abide with you now and always.

Breathe in and out slowly, with connected and relaxing breaths, at a gentle rate that will energize your being, but at the same time not make you dizzy.

Survey your body from the tip of your toes to the crown of your head to ensure that you are calm, comfortable, relaxed and quiet. As you survey your body, release tension from each muscle and relax, leaving all the cares and concerns of the world behind. Realize that you are Spirit and it is time to devote your energy to Spirit.

[Pause for two minutes as you survey your body, releasing tension to move into the state of relaxation. Take as much time as you feel necessary. As you prepare, realize that relaxation is challenging the mind.]

Universal Love

Now that you are in a state of total relaxation, focus on the area of the heart. Take a deep breath as you contemplate Love. Concentrate on all that is Love and nothing else. Fill your mind with complete and absolute Love. Think about a special place where you feel the presence of Love, or perhaps a special person, or a child, a morning walk, the sunrise or perhaps a quiet church sanctuary as you fill your mind with feelings of pure and absolute Love. As you breathe, feel the calm and transforming power of Love. With every breath, let only Love surround your entire being. Everything is Love and there is nothing else.

Feel the peace and calm that is carried on the wings of Love. As you breathe, feel the transformation unfolding within. Feel the brilliance of this love grow within you. Feel the glow of Love grow as a brilliant green Light, emanating from the centre of your being in your heart. Feel the energy of Love. You are Love.

[Pause as you feel the embrace of the energy of Love as it shines from your heart and as you breathe, feel the glow grow and expand.]

Take time to see the brilliance of this Light as it surrounds your entire body. Feel the Light as it fills your aura. You shine. You glisten. Every cell of your being is glowing. You are a Light, glowing and glistening, more brilliant than the sun.

[Pause as you feel the glory of the Light. See the power and magnificence of the Light as you shine.]

As you stand inside this Light, shining brilliantly, look around. All is Light. In the distance, you will see a golden glow, gold bathed in a magnificent green, shining with every colour of the rainbow, surrounded by a pure, brilliant white light. Light is everywhere. Feel the Love emanating from that Light. Walk towards that golden glow.

[Pause for a moment as you enter the Light. In your meditation, you have journeyed to the realm of Love, the realm of the Creator. Bow your head to receive of the blessings of the Light. Feel the calm within you as you rest in the comfort of this healing Light.]

Prayer

Divine Creator, I give thanks for the blessing of your all-embracing Light. Awaken every cell within me with the touch of your Love, which shines from your being. Amen.

[Pause as you receive the touch of the Creator.]

Breathe in the Light that surrounds you. As you breathe, feel that wondrous golden Light enter your body. Take time now to relax in this shining presence and let the Light flood into your being. As you breathe, feel the Light enter your lungs, and as you slowly exhale, feel the wondrous Light gush through your veins, into your blood stream, travelling through your entire body, slowly, from the tip of your toes to your crown of your head. See it enter every organ. See it touch every cell. As it touches each cell, feel it as it invigorates, transforms and heals. Feel the touch and power of the Creator enlightening every cell of your being. Examine your body. Ensure that each cell of your body is touched by that Love and Light, energized and glowing. Feel the calm and peace and Love that is beyond all words.

In patience, receive all that you have been given. Take time for each cell of your being to be transformed by this elixir, a healing balm. Feel this taking place within your entire being, in this very moment.

[Pause for five minutes...]

It is now time to bid farewell. Before you leave, in your heart give thanks for all that you have received. You have been honoured with the gift of Love flowing from the Creator's Light. You have felt the peace, calm and joy. Give thanks for the healing manifested by the Light. Give your thanks for all that you have received.

It is now time to return, to journey back once again to that wonderful, green Light emanating from your heart. As you enter that wonderful, green Light, allow it to fill your heart, your entire being, with all that you need.

Keep all that you have received from the Light of the Creator as a gift of enlightenment for your journey through life. Remember that the Light of the Creator shines from within and it is always there whenever you choose to open the door.

It is now time to return to the consciousness of your physical body and the realm that surrounds you. When you are ready to return, gently open your eyes.

Prayer

Divine Creator, I give thanks for the blessing of your Light. I give thanks for the blessing of your Love and Truth that shines from your being. I give thanks for the blessing of your healing energy.

I pray that you will guide me as I walk the path of transformation, as I search to embrace all that I am, on my journey onward and upward seeking the eternal embrace of your Light. Amen.

Meditation

The Breath

My Spirit spoke to me of the breath, of prana, and taking it into the area of the heart.

"Breathe deeply and fully and be blessed. Breathe in that chi, the vital energy of life and Light and Love and receive that power to expand your heart centre. Feel the luminous green Light glowing within, with power, magnificence and glory, rising up to the crown, growing to encompass your entire being, protecting you, and expanding to touch all that surrounds you."

As you breathe, command the energy that emerges from within and repeat this most loved prayer.

The Light of the Spirit surrounds me.
The Love of the Spirit transforms me.
The Truth of the Spirit protects me.
Wherever I AM
I shine with the brilliance of my Spirit.
The spark of the Eternal.
Amen.

Reflection

Carving the Way

You have journeyed long and far and now you are ready. It is time for you to look to the other side of life, to that glimmering place of Light beyond this physical realm. As time marches on, and you are challenged in different ways, you are faced with opportunities to transcend this realm. The choices that you make are the opportunities to embrace the essence of life.

In this physical existence, which you have created, you have walked deep into a valley surrounded by illusions, and with the passing of time your eyes no longer recognize what is real, nor can you see the pathway which leads beyond the shadows and out of the valley.

There is a part of you that always seeks to rise above these illusions, innately searching for the pathway back to the place of Light. The challenges that you face each day are the opportunities to once again open your eyes so that you can find the pathway. These challenges will unfetter you so you can embark on that journey onward and upward into Light.

As you encounter challenges along the way, you can choose to either face them with Love and Truth or walk away. The pathway of Love and Truth offers the realization that they are indeed the foundation of your being. All that is real is founded upon Love and Truth.

As you choose to embrace the way of Love and Truth, the doorway, which transcends this realm of illusion, will open, revealing the way out of the valley of shadows, where you can once again embrace the Light. This Light is the essence of life. It is the Light that existed from the beginning of time, and shall always be. As you choose to embrace Love and Truth, this Light will shine from within so you can live and grow as one with this Light, for you are Light. Every cell of your being is filled with Light. It is choice that will enable your Light to shine once again with brilliance, which is who you are.

Remember always to choose the way of Love and Truth. It is the path which takes you out of the valley of shadows to the place where there are no illusions.

It takes the strength and courage of a warrior to travel this pathway. The warrior wields a sword of Truth, carving the pathway out of the valley onward and upward into the all-embracing eternal Light that is life.

Fear not, for you are strong. You have the courage to embark on this journey. Realize that it is your choice, a choice that no other can make for you. You are the one who will gain. What will you gain? It is joy in your heart, for all are meant to be happy. It is eternal bliss. Remember that bliss is the natural state of your being. You are the only one who can choose this path and you have the strength and courage to do it. You only need to choose it. Each step takes you one step closer. You are the one responsible for the state of your Spirit. Everyone is responsible for the state of their Spirit. Life is a journey of personal responsibility; therefore, choose, for you are worth it. You are the potter, so choose to sculpt your own life.

Reflection

What Is Love?

Love is acceptance.
Love has no condition.
Love has no expectation.
Love holds no judgment.

How do you Love?
Love self first.
Love self so fully and completely
That you overflow with such joy
That embraces all that you touch.

Illumination

Rock of Ages

For I will walk into the fires of death
With true resolve
Unshaken and unmoved in who I am.
For I am the embodiment of Love and Truth
Unwavering
And in this I will have my being
Unto the ends of eternity.
Amen.

Reflection

Love

Within the world today, many talk of Love, each having a different perspective or concept.

What is the greatest form of Love? Love, like blood, is the essence of life. It is a vehicle which feeds the Spirit, your Spirit. When there is a state of balance within your being, Love flows. When Love flows, joy fills your being.

It is true that there are many forms of Love. There is familial Love felt between brother and sister or parents and children. There is Love between friends. There is Love between husband and wife. There is Love for a pet and for inanimate objects such as cars and houses. More commonly, many interchange the word "Love" with "sex," and hold firmly to the perception that "sex" is Love. Under these circumstances, experiencing sexuality has no direct relationship with the greatest form of Love.

Such Love is the essence of life. It is freely available to everyone. It is this form of Love that connects all as one. When you are embraced by this Love, you feel no judgment. You feel total and unconditional acceptance for everyone, including yourself.

It is a great challenge to embrace such Love, for judgment and rejection come easily, especially of the self. If you can truly Love yourself, then you will find it easy to Love others.

By understanding fear, you can gain a better understanding of Love. Fear is a function of your mind. It is created so you remain in a place of perceived comfort. For example, if you know you must face a certain challenge, your mind creates fear, based on reason, logic, science or whatever else, trying to prevent you from accepting this challenge. The mind will even go as far as making your body tremble. Although you may know the Truth within, society accepts logic, reason and science to remain within a comfort zone. Society rejects the concept of "feelings" and accepting the way of the Spirit. Instead, it accepts fear and stagnates.

Another common example is the fear of "lack." No one wants to feel the lack of anything, so many go out to buy and horde. It's the same with nations. Many countries have a perception that they must freely and abundantly covet their neighbours' properties and establish policies of domination, which sometimes lead to wars, and loss of life.

Fear can have great power if you allow it to manifest. Love can be viewed as the opposite of fear. It is the Love for self and humanity that dissolves fear. As the heart chakra opens, it is this Love that emerges. It is your choice that will enable this Love to manifest. It is this Love that is described as "spiritual" that connects all as one with the Creator of life.

Lesson 48

Fear and Love

A student asked a question regarding fear. "Why are we attracted to the things that we fear the most?" The things that you fear always seem to come your way. You do everything possible to avoid situations, but inevitably they come, again and again. Why?

These things come your way because of unresolved issues that you must face sooner or later on your journey. These things come your way because of their potential to make you strong. Strength gives you the ability to face greater challenges in the future. You soon realize that resolved issues open doors to a greater reality.

These answers tell us WHY, but there is another question that should also be addressed. HOW do you face your fears? Have you ever wondered if there is a method or process?

When you are faced with fears, most times you tend to react with instinct. In the animal kingdom, fear brings aggression. Aggression sometimes brings hurt and pain and even death; thus, it is not the best approach to take. Perhaps you should seek your inner guidance and then react accordingly.

What is the basic Truth that can be followed in this situation? As students of life and seekers of Truth, your quest is for the understanding of life and its wonders. Truth comes in many ways and forms.

To understand the Truth regarding the facing of fears, you may gain wisdom from the following story of a man called Standing Elk, an aboriginal from New Jersey, USA. Standing Elk was sixty-one years of age when he told this tale, one of his personal life experiences and it is being related with his permission.

Although some of the concepts and ideas in this true story may not be commonly accepted beliefs, there is much to gather from it if you are willing to open your hearts and minds and seek the Truth.

Some years ago, Standing Elk moved to a new home in the desert area of Utah. There he had much land, where there were many snakes on his property. When you talk of snakes, many cringe with fear. When you think of places in the world where snakes are large and poisonous, the fear becomes even greater.

He moved to Utah with his wife and young children and he feared for their safety, for their lives and for himself. He did not know what to do, for they couldn't stay indoors all day. One day, he had counted over fifty snakes in the yard.

First, he prayed for guidance, and then he sought the help of the wise man of his tribe. The wise man told him that he should talk to the snakes and make them a fair deal. Aboriginal people have a great connection with Earth and the animal kingdom. Modern society is now learning about this connection, which the indigenous people of North America have been aware of for eons. Perhaps this is an example of eternal truths that apply not only to aboriginals, but to all humankind.

Standing Elk went out into the bush and spoke to the snakes. Talking to snakes is not a simple process. Aboriginals know of ways to connect with the animal kingdom. Their technique is similar to a deep meditative trance used when connecting with Spirit guides. How they do this is not important. Perhaps in time, as you grow, you may also understand more of this connection. You will understand more of your connection with the entire animal kingdom, with the earth and all of life.

Standing Elk asked the snakes to stay out of the yard during the daytime. They could hunt there at night, but not during the day. And they were not to bite his family. In return, he would not kill them. This seemed to be a fair deal. The next day, there were no snakes in the yard. He almost stepped on one near the fence at the far end of the yard, but it did not bite him. It just slithered away. It sounds far-fetched, but it's true.

Here is another true story. In the Caribbean, there are many poisonous snakes. One day, a woman accidentally pulled a deadly coral snake from the root of an anthurium plant with her bare hand. Anthuriums produce beautiful flowers and thrive in a damp environment filled with rotted wood. Snakes also love such an environment. The old woman loved her garden. When she realized what she had in her hands, the old woman dropped the snake and ran. Later, her son found the snake and destroyed it. There were young children in the house who played in the yard, and such venomous creatures were dangerous. Because of the fear of these creatures, and their lethal poison, aggression was the natural reaction.

What can you learn from these two stories regarding fears, and facing them? When faced with the fear of snakes, the instinctive reaction is to use aggression and kill the creatures. Many, however, have realized that humankind shares the earth equally with all creatures; likewise, all creatures share this earth equally with humankind, all as part of the great puzzle and symbiosis of life. Each has a unique task, a unique place in the grand garden. All creatures deserve equal Love and respect with the cohesion of creation.

It is said that the opposite of fear is Love and acceptance. Standing Elk did not use aggression created by fear. Because of his understanding of the animal kingdom and the garden of Earth, he chose to act with Love, respect and acceptance. He chose to negotiate instead of removing part of the grand puzzle. And he negotiated successfully.

These are two stories about facing fear. When you are faced with fear, do you react with aggression or respond with Love?

How does this relate to your own life and your spirituality? All face a multitude of fears every day. You may fear your boss. You may fear busy traffic. You may fear the lack of abundance (not having sufficient money, food, clothing, etc.). You may fear abandonment. You may fear not being accepted. You may fear war. The list goes on and on. Take a moment to think about it. Remember what comes to mind for you may need to face it later.

What you fear eventually finds you, over and over again. You can't hide. You have all seen this. What do you do? HOW do you address your fears?

Would you continue to hide from them or would you face them and conquer them once and for all? Would you face them head on? Would you react instinctively with aggression? Would you explore how you can dissolve fear with Love?

Standing Elk faced his fear of the snakes by applying Love for all of creatures. You can do the same. You can apply Love to all situations. Love has a mighty transforming power. Every situation you can think of, there is a way to apply Love to dissolve the fear.

If all the leaders of the world understood the relationship between <u>Love</u> and <u>Fear,</u> and applied the principle of Love instead of reacting instinctively with aggression, can you not taste the world peace that would result? Choose to explore your fears and dissolve them with your own power to manifest Love here on Earth. Amen.

Prayer

Prayer for Strength

Fill my heart with thankfulness for the kindness I have experienced in my life. Fill my heart with the desire to return such kindness as I feel the joy and Love within me.

Fill my heart with the desire to choose a path upon which my fears may be dissolved.

Fill me with strength to face the fears that befall me.

Fill my heart with courage to replace such fears with Love, clearing a path to the Light that is the essence of life. Amen.

Reflection

Replace Fear with Love

Have you not seen the Truth?
You have been called again and again.
The words you have heard
The words of your heart.

Stand up and be strong.
Look to the Light and seek the way.
The Light shines for you.
The Light flows within your veins.
The Light which dissolves all fear.

Rise up and be strong.
Walk forth a victor.
You have been challenged.

How long will you remain a prisoner?
The time is now.
Walk free.

Let the rains fall upon you and drench you with Love.
Love will cleanse.
Love will set your Spirit free.
Amen.

Reflection

It Is Who You Are

It is who you are.
Have you forgotten
All of this is you?

What you feel
What you think
Your totality.

Time grows like rust
Blinds your eyes like scales
Deafens your ears like wax.

Choose now and forgive yourself.
Cleanse yourself.
Remove the scales of time.

Remove the scales of hurt and disappointment.
Remove the scales of stagnation.
Remove the scales of fear.

You know who you are, the *word*.
You are the embodiment of Light.
You know your *name*.

Awaken once again to the Light
For you are a warrior
And journey onward and upward.
Amen.

Reflection

Six

As above, So below
Trinity in duality,
Choose thou.

Who are you?
Look within
And know the truth.

Know from whence you have your being.
Know the source of your life.
Know the power of your breath.

What do you create?
What do you choose?
What do you manifest?

Know who you are.
Born of Light
You are Light.

A creation of Truth.
It is all Truth.
You are Truth.

Choose! It is all choice.
You have the free will to be all that you are.
As above, so below.

Lesson 49

Challenge Yourself

Even during the greatest challenge, be prepared to manifest the Light from your heart. You will be challenged.

Likewise, challenge yourself to embrace the Light from the centre of your being in all your interactions. Face your challenge with a challenge.

What is the greatest challenge? It is the mind, which seeks dominion. Fear, old patterns, anger, lack of abundance, ego, pride, revenge, etc., will all seek to manifest their way. These are the tools of the mind. You have yielded in the past. In the past, your mind had control.

Therefore challenge yourself, your mind and your body, indeed your totality to be the manifestation of Love. Take the time to pray, meditate and embrace the Spirit. When the Spirit is in command, Love will flow freely from the centre of your being. Love will become the way of your being. Love will become the transforming force. It is the desire of Spirit to manifest Love in each moment.

Lesson 50

In Each Moment

Even during the greatest challenge there is always an answer. Know that Truth and Love will protect and guide you. Therefore, embrace all the facets of your being and be prepared, a warrior of Light, manifesting Love and Truth in words, thoughts and actions, in each moment. It is the desire of your Spirit.

Lesson 51

A Firm Foundation

What is your house built upon?

Have you been swayed by the winds (of change) as you followed the call of bliss on the road which leads to Light?

Is your Spirit built upon the fountain of Truth that flows from within? Have you searched the depths of your heart for Truth, which leads you away from the shadows, and towards the Light that is life eternal?

Seek life.
Feed it with Love.
Let it grow upon the firm foundation of Truth.
Building many mansions so magnificent and glorious.
Growing and transcending.
A glimmering Spirit of joy.
A jewel of Light.
Gleaming onward and upward into eternity.

Lesson 52

The Journey of the Heart

Life is about feelings.
What you feel within is the voice of a higher consciousness.
It is the voice of your Spirit.
It is a voice that speaks within the heart.

The heart is a doorway.
Through this door is a bridge to the higher realms.

The unity of hearts is the unity of Spirit.
It is an all-embracing consciousness.
It unites all as one with Love.

When you embrace life, you embrace your heart.
It is an embrace of the Spirit.
The journey of the heart is a journey of Truth.
It is a journey of Love.
It is Love which unites all as one.

Spiritual oneness is an all-embracing Light.
The Light of the Creator of life.

Reflection

The Earth Experience

In the beginning, you were one
And will always be one
Light
A spark of God.

In the beginning, you were one
Now you are two
Spirit and flesh
In duality.

In the beginning, you were one
Now you are three
Mind, flesh and Spirit
The trinity.

In the beginning, you were one
Now you are six
Three above and three below
Trinity in duality.

In the beginning, you were one
Now you are seven
Spirit touching the flesh in seven places
Bridged by Love.

In the beginning, you were one
Now, who are you?
Each one above as three
As above so below.

In the beginning, you were one
And who you are is your choice.

Illumination

Life Is a Song

Choose the path of growth each day
Walk the road of life this way
The Creator is with you each brick you lay

Being all that you are, for this you long.
You are Spirit and in this you are strong
The way of the Creator is your song
Amen

Illumination

Sing a New Song

You have journeyed long and far
Seeking to be all that you are

To once again sing that old song
For you have chosen to be strong

Your heart as your guide
With Love at your side.

Truth is your shield
None will make you yield

As a warrior of Light
Your home is now in sight.
Amen.

Reflection

Love

Learn to accept Love.
Learn to give Love.
And therein you will find life.

Life is held in the crucible called Love.
Open it and you will find all that you seek.
You will find bliss.

Go to the centre of your being
And when you get there, stop.
Listen for the voice of the Spirit.

There you will find guidance.
You will find Truth.
There you will find the doorway to God's Love.
Amen.

Reflection

Know What Is Love

It is the lifeblood of your Spirit.
It is the energy that gives life to your Spirit.
Love is the energy of growth and change.

How do I express the Love from within?
First I must learn to Love myself so completely
That my joy overflows to embrace you.
Love flows through all and connects all as one.

Illumination

Find Your Centre

Breathe
Slow down
Relax
Find your centre.

Feel Spirit within.
Spirit awaits your call.

To speak with you
To share with you
To share Love
To share Truth
To unite as one with the flesh.

To fill your consciousness with Light
To open the door to the Light
To embrace you with Light
To awaken you to the Light.

That you may feel the Light
And be the Light
And connect with the Light
And journey with the Light
Onward and upward.
Amen.

Meditation

I Love

I am Love.
I am guided by Love.
I will manifest Love.

I live my life with Love.
I choose the path of Love.
I create with Love.

I embrace all with Love.
Amen.

Reflection

Feel Each Word

When you pray and meditate, feel each *word*.
Each *word* holds energy or vibration.
Embrace this energy.
Synchronize with the vibration.

Each chakra responds to a different *word*.
Each chakra responds to a different note.
Feel the music of the spheres.
Dance to the music of the Light.

The tree of life shines.
It is who you are.
Amen.

(Please refer to the sections on the word in chapter three.)

Meditation

The Words of the Spirit

As you contemplate your activities from times gone by, seek understanding. Seek acceptance. Seek Truth.

Find the correlation with the sacred "tree of light" that is within, that part of your being that is illuminated, where Spirit touches the flesh.

That which brought discord, seek out the energy, the chakra, from where it emerged.

Seek the *word* that will restore balance. Let this *word* guide your intentions as you make new choices. New choices will bring transformation.

"Prayerfully" approach all your activities, so your choices may be guided by intentions based on the words of the Spirit.

(Please refer to the sections on the word in chapter three.)

Illumination

When Transformation Happens

You will feel it.
Bliss.
You will dance with a joy that is eternal.

You will feel a shift in your being.
You will be in command of your being.
You will command the mind to be silent and Spirit will emerge.

You will feel the desire to manifest your heart.
You will feel the desire to manifest your Truth.

You will have an attitude that is positive and hopeful.
You will embrace all that is life.
You will know all things are possible.

You will shine from every cell of your being, with every word, every
thought and every action.

You will choose.
You will manifest your power.
You will be all that you are.
Amen.

Meditation

The Tree of Life

I live upon bread of life.
I feel my Spirit.
I will overcome the flesh.
I Love all that I am.
I speak all that is Truth.
I see all that I am.

For
I am Spirit
Manifesting in oneness
With the flesh
All that I AM.
Amen.

Conclusion

The Secret

Finding Your Purpose

It is your innate desire to embrace the fullness of life and find the place of bliss which your Spirit calls home. On the journey to that place, realize that it is your life which you command, and you have the free will to choose the path you follow.

Choose to meditate daily. Let your meditations become the source of your strength that guides your aspirations. Choose to unite in oneness with the totality of your being. It is an embrace where Spirit and flesh become one. It is an embrace where Spirit is in command of the mind. It is the secret and innate desire of your Spirit and your true purpose.

As you meditate, seek to find this place of Truth within, the place of Love, your power centre, and carry it with you on your journey of experience within these three dimensions, here on Earth. Know that your purpose is to find and embrace this place for it is the source of your inner Light.

Know the secret. You hold the secret within. You are the secret. You are the answer. Your Spirit is the answer. Manifesting the desires of your Spirit is the answer to all questions. Oneness with Spirit is your home. Choose now to embark on this journey for it is your true purpose. The answer to all questions lies within, for you are Truth, Love and bliss. It is all within and although it is so simple, it is the sacred secret of eternal life. Open your eyes and you will see.

Meditation for Creating Bliss

Bliss

Know that your home is a state of being
Where you are in oneness with life,
Here and in the realms beyond.
It is the state of bliss.

§

Know that you are Spirit first.
Feel the desires of your Spirit.
Express the desires of your Spirit.

Manifest the desires of Spirit in this realm.
Experience the bliss of your Spirit
And let your heart be the guide.

Let Love be your guide.
Let Truth be your guide.
Let joy be your home.

Let the Spirit within be your guide.
Let Spirit be your Light and your life
Here and in the realms beyond
Now and forever more.
Amen.

Reflection

Here on Earth

As you reflect on your own lives, you see that every religion believes in life beyond life and the continuous existence of the Spirit. As Christians or Buddhists or Hindus or Muslims or whatever you feel you are, life beyond this physical life is a fundamental component of your belief system and the way of being.

In ancient times, the one who walked in Nazareth offered the pattern which many observe today. According to tradition, for forty days beyond physical death he was seen in this physical realm, here on the earth, which you are a part of. Although it was many, many years ago, the very dust upon which he walked still exists today, for it was scattered by the winds everywhere and still lays upon the ground beneath your feet. Remember that dust does not die but forms the substance of life here on this planet. Some of this dust nourished plants and trees, the food which you ate. Some became the bricks that form the buildings within which you live, as shelter or as your life. Your lives, past and present, are so connected physically, as well as in the Truth that was set forth by the pattern of the ancient Nazarene Master. Your Spirit continues beyond the physical world, then journeys home after forty days.

Such Truth gives purpose to your lives, and faith in Truth forms the foundation of your way of life here on Earth. You are here not only because of this faith and Truth, but because of who you are. You are Spirit which temporarily found a place, a home here on Earth, to one day return to your joy and glory, your true home in the realms beyond.

Message of Transcendence

Dust to Dust and Light to Light

The time will come when you will choose to return home. You must realize that it is no sacrifice.

It is a time when your work here in the physical realm has been accomplished. It is only at that time you will choose to leave this physical realm and journey to your true home.

Even if you are not consciously aware of it, it is intrinsic to your being. Spirit knows your desire, purpose and accomplishments. Spirit is aware of the grand plan for your whole life, here and beyond.

When you choose to leave, it will be the right time, from the perspective of your Spirit. There is nothing to fear.

At this stage of your journey, you will realize the benefits of being here and the purpose of continuing your journey onward and upward into eternal Light.

You will return home a new being, one filled with joy, blessed with Love and Truth and empowered by the Light of your Spirit.

Message of Transcendence

It Is Not Goodbye

It is a good time.
In Truth, there is no better time.
I have done all that I need to do.
And now it is time for me to move on.

No need for you to be unhappy.
It is a time for all to rejoice.
It is a time to celebrate this life.

For such is life.
And life continues.
That which I am still exists.
That which I am has always existed.
That which I am will continue to exist.

What is this life that you see?
I have gathered this dust around me to manifest the essence of my Spirit here in this physical realm, so that I can Love, so that I can create.

Suffer yourself no more.
Know that the physical is only an illusion.
What you perceive as life in the physical realm is only an illusion.
In Truth, Spirit reaches from beyond into this physical world.

When you see this Truth
When you live this Truth
Only then will you find meaning in life.

Choose to create a life of joy and you will walk this path of Truth.
Walk your Truth and you will create joy in your life.
This is the way to fulfill the purpose of your Spirit.

Message of Transcendence

Internment

It is not the end
For I will see you again.

Fire and smoke will take that which I no longer need.
The smoke will become one with all smoke.
It will rise to a sky that is clear and blue.
There, to remain always.
Be joyful in this.

The dust will be freed to become dust once again.
I have given it freedom once more with thanks.
It will flow with the pure rivers of water from high upon the mountain top.
It will unite once again with its mother, the Earth.
To her, I give thanks.
For she shared of herself without condition or expectation,
That I might experience Love and joy
Founded upon Truth
On a path of oneness with life.

On the journey of my Spirit into life.

Message of Transcendence

Just Wave Hello

It is not the end.
For I will see you again.

With this, leave your tears behind.
Let it become one with the rivers
Then cry no more.

It is not goodbye.
Just wave hello.

For I will sing with you again.
A song of Love
A song of Truth
A song of joy.

All that was created in Spirit, lives, always.
All that was created in Love, lives, always.
All that was created in Truth, lives, always.
All that was created in joy, lives, always.

United as one in Love, and Truth and in joy.

So now, I journey once again into life
Thus, my journey into Light.
Amen.

Appendix A

World Meditation

Your state of being at this very moment is who you are. What do you manifest? Know that you are a Light shining in the darkness of existence. What do you radiate? What do you give to the world? What do you give to humanity? What do you give to existence?

It is by being all that you are that you give of yourself and for yourself. When you meditate, embrace all that you are. Radiate all that you are. You are the heavens. You are the "I AM." You are Truth. You are Love. You will transcend. You will create. You will survive. Let this Light radiate from the depths of your being to embrace all of existence.

Radiate Love. Radiate Truth. Radiate peace. Radiate hope. Radiate gentleness. Radiate compassion. Radiate kindness. Radiate your inner Light, which is joy.

As you meditate and share all that you are with the world, pray that others will join in unity to strengthen this pathway of sharing. Know the Truth, for those in need will feel what you share. As you feel the power of transformation within you, pray that it will ignite hope for transformation within the world. Amen.

Meditation for World Peace

This meditation has been designed for the outdoors using the sounds of nature and the music from the realms. If you so choose, this meditation can also be done with a group.

Take the time now to become centred, so you may focus on channelling eternal Love and Light.

Prepare to unite your heart, mind and Spirit in oneness with the world.

Be at peace. Feel the Love of the realms embrace your heart. Feel the Light of life shine from within.

Fill your heart with thankfulness. Fill your heart with the desire to embrace the angels. Fill your heart with the desire to embrace all who seek to manifest the Light. Fill your heart with the desire for guidance and inspiration that Love may be channelled to all of humankind. Fill your heart with the desire for the protection offered by the angels. Feel the embrace of the Light of protection as it surrounds you.

Call upon the guardians of this world for an infusion of Divine Energy so the desire for peace may fill the heart and minds of all, and unconditional Love will prevail.

Prepare now to channel the divine energies.

Prayer

May the petitions of my Spirit and of all Spirits, and the meditations of my heart and of all hearts bring healing Light to all who seek. In my heart, I petition the Creator to bestow Love and Light and protection and guidance at this most holy time. Amen.

Sit comfortably, with your back gently erect and hands loosely placed. Take a deep, relaxing breath, and exhale slowly and fully. As you exhale, relax.

Take another deep, relaxing breath, and exhale slowly and fully. As you exhale, relax.

In your heart, give thanks to the Creator for the opportunity to share in this occasion of healing.

Seek out the force of Light that it may shine brilliantly within, and within all people.

Close your eyes and relax.

Take a deep breath and as you exhale, relax.

During this meditation, you will become filled with so much energy that your cup will overflow, spilling upon the earth to bring Love, and peace, harmony and healing to all.

Seventh Chakra

The crowning glory of your reality is at hand as you reach beyond to unite in oneness with the eternal Light. Open your heart that you may feel the presence of the Creator, as the eternal Light now surrounds you. Feel the warmth of Love only possible with the presence of the Creator as an immense beam of Light pouring down upon you.

As you breathe, feel the burning purity of the white Light surrounding your crown and see it snake its way through your being, counter-clockwise, touching each chakra, each energy centre, brightening, purifying and enlightening. Take the time to breathe this in and allow it to permeate every cell of your being.

1. Take a deep breath, hold and exhale slowly.
2. Take a deep breath, hold and exhale slowly.
3. Take a deep breath, hold and exhale slowly.

See this Light dance and glitter as it snakes its way through your entire being, touching every organ and cell. Feel the Light as it activates the endocrine system, releasing healing hormones into your bloodstream.

Sixth Chakra

It is now time to journey to the area of the third eye and place your focus between the brows. There you will feel the brilliant indigo Light shining, shimmering and spinning.

Within this Light, you can see glorious shapes of stars and snowflakes. You can see white surrounded by pinkish purple, all filled with a golden glow. See these dance and shimmer, as this area becomes brighter and stronger as you breathe.

1. Take a deep breath, hold and exhale slowly.
2. Take a deep breath, hold and exhale slowly.
3. Take a deep breath, hold and exhale slowly.

Prayer

My heart is filled with thankfulness for the touch of eternal Love. My heart is filled with desire for a blessing for everyone on the planet, that eternal Love, the fabric of existence, will encompass all. My heart is filled with desire for guidance to a place where mind, body and Spirit are embraced by this wondrous elixir, the wonderful glory of life and Light. My heart is filled with the desire for all to feel the touch of the indigo Light opening and clearing the way to a new reality. Amen.

Fifth Chakra

It is now time to focus on the throat. See this area glow with a brilliant blue Light. As you breathe, see the fifth chakra grow more and more brilliant and clearer. Feel the power of Truth manifest within your being.

1. Take a deep breath, hold and exhale slowly.
2. Take a deep breath, hold and exhale slowly.
3. Take a deep breath, hold and exhale slowly.

Prayer

My heart is filled with thankfulness for the touch of eternal Love. My heart is filled with thankfulness for the joy that it brings. I petition the Creator for the embrace of Truth that it may become a guiding force in the hearts of all who seek, to see and feel Love more clearly on the pathway of life. I petition my higher self to reveal the secrets that lie within my soul, so I may find the doorway to my true reality.

I petition the Creator of all life that I may find the strength and courage to walk my path, living the Truth which emanates from my being as I journey onward into the glorious Light of life. Amen.

First Chakra

Take three deep breaths, and as you breathe, focus on the base of the spine and the colour red. With each breath, see this area become brighter and clearer with the purity of a red glow.

1. Take a deep breath, hold and exhale slowly.
2. Take a deep breath, hold and exhale slowly.
3. Take a deep breath, hold and exhale slowly.

Prayer

I give thanks to the Creator for the pathway of eternal Love that is experienced here on Earth. I give thanks to the earth for the opportunity to partake in her abundance, gentle nurturing and Spirit of growth. I give thanks to the Creator for an infusion of the energy of Love and Light so all who walk this road of life may choose to manifest peace and harmony. Amen.

Third Chakra

Now it is time to focus on the solar plexus. See this area shine with a yellow glow. See it grow brilliant and clear with each breath. Feel the power of the Creator of life within your being.

1. Take a deep breath, hold and exhale slowly.
2. Take a deep breath, hold and exhale slowly.
3. Take a deep breath, hold and exhale slowly.

Prayer
My heart is filled with thankfulness for the Love and Light of the Creator of life. I petition the Creator of life for guidance along the way that all may find strength and courage to manifest peace and Love on the journey through life. Amen.

Second Chakra

At this time, breathe into the sacral area. As you breathe, see this area fill with a glow of orange. With each breath, see the glow grow more and more brilliant.

1. Take a deep breath, hold and exhale slowly.
2. Take a deep breath, hold and exhale slowly.
3. Take a deep breath, hold and exhale slowly.

Prayer
My heart is filled with thankfulness for the Love and Light that the Creator of life has bestowed upon this realm of physical existence. My heart is filled with thankfulness for the opportunity to walk upon this realm of existence as a beacon of Light, brightening the way of all those who seek the path of Love and creativity. I petition the Creator of life that my cup and all cups may be filled to the

brim with peace and harmony, spilling over to all of humankind. Amen.

Fourth Chakra

Now it is time to focus on the heart. See this area shine with a brilliant glow of green. And as you breathe, see it grow more and more brilliant.

1. Take a deep breath, hold and exhale slowly. See this green grow and encompass the world. In Spirit, in Love, in Truth, you are all of one heart.
2. Take a deep breath, hold and exhale slowly. See this green grow more and more brilliant as it expands out.
3. Take a deep breath, hold and exhale slowly. See this green grow more and more brilliant, expanding out as far as you can reach. Within the green, see a shimmering pinkish purple as it reaches around the globe.

Know within your heart that there are many like you who are meditating right now, sending their Love and Light around the globe. Become one in Love and Light.

Prayer

My heart is filled with thankfulness for eternal Light, for the free will to partake of that divine elixir called Love, uniting the entire world in peace and harmony as one.

My heart is filled with so much Love that every entity on this planet feels the touch today. The seeds of Love become firmly planted in the heart of everyone, ensuring a future of peace and harmony, one that will become the inheritance of the children of this time. Amen.

Healing the Earth

Feel the energy flow through you, from the base of your spine, snaking its way to the crown, energizing and filling your entire being with so much Light you shine as the Light flows out of your crown to spill upon the earth beneath you. See it enter and make its way to the core, the centre of the earth.

Feel this Light flow through your being, making its way to the centre of the earth. Feel this Light grow and glow as like minds around the globe do, as well. Feel the core of the earth glow brilliantly with the blue and green Light that all like minds are channelling.

Join in oneness at that momentous time, as Love and Truth infuse at the centre, the core, making it glow brilliantly.

As the core glows, it gleams outwards, shining more and more brilliantly, channelling that Love outward and upward, and again making its way to the surface.

As this energy, this Love and Light makes its way to the surface, the entire world glows.

Feel Asia glow with a brilliant red.

Feel Africa glow with a brilliant orange.

Feel North America glow with a wondrous yellow.

Feel South America glow with a magnificent green.

Feel Europe glow with a joyous blue.

Feel Australia glow with a shimmering indigo.

Feel the Arctic glow with a glorious violet.

Feel the entire world glow with a rainbow of colours shining with this Divine Light, as it touches every molecule and living thing.

Feel the energy as it returns through the base of your spine. As you unite in oneness and breathe, magnify the Love and Light and Truth you emanate. All who are ready to receive may breathe it into their being, energizing and harmonizing as it touches their Spirit, enlightening, transforming seeds to manifest, now and always.

One in Spirit

You are now one in Spirit. You are one in Love, and one in Truth. Fill your heart with the desire that the energy you emanate will assist Mother Earth with her adjustments, and the changes that must take place will occur with calm and gentility. As you breathe, feel the entire earth as it now shines with the pinkish purple glow of Love and peace. Take a moment to breathe in and feel the energy and Light that surround you.

Breathe in this wondrous light as it returns from the core of the earth, making its way up to the surface, through your base chakra, snaking its way back, clockwise, touching every energy centre within your being, balancing, enriching, purifying, healing and wending its way through the crown, up and back to its source.

Take a deep breath, filling your being with the fullness of Love.

Prayer

My heart is filled with thankfulness for the healing brought to my being and the entire world. My heart is filled with thankfulness for the opportunity to facilitate this healing by being a channel of Love and Light.

My heart is filled with the desire that every heart that has received the touch will embark on a new journey of Love and Light, bringing peace and harmony to all of existence.

My heart is filled with thankfulness for the opportunity to travel through this portal to a new beginning, one embraced by Love and Light. Amen.

Closing

Take a moment to commune with the Creator, for soon it will be time to return to the physical realm. Take a deep breath and as you exhale, allow your consciousness to return to the physical realm.

Feel the energized air embrace your body like a gentle kiss upon your face.

Take a deep but gentle breath and as you slowly exhale, become conscious of the sensations of your physicality. When you are ready, you may open your eyes, feeling alert, energized and loved.

Prayer
My heart is filled with thankfulness for the opportunity to share in the eternal Love and Light of the Creator. Amen.

Appendix B

Light Buds – Seeds That Grow

1. The secrets of life are like seeds. Seeds of Light that you plant within. You nurture them and they blossom to illumine you.
2. Justify yourself by what you know and feel about yourself, for it is upon the foundation of Love and Truth that you have your being.
3. You are like a flower: Blossom in every way.
4. The desires of Spirit are seeds of joy. Plant them and they will grow.
5. Plant seeds of Light. They will grow and blossom into bliss.
6. The nature of your Spirit is to shine with its brilliance, which is bliss.
7. Create joy out of each situation for it is the desire of your Spirit.
8. Let choice navigate your path into Light. Choose what will bring you joy.
9. When you bring joy to your being, you manifest the desires of your own Spirit.
10. Love begins at home. It is the body that is the temple or home of the Spirit. Love is acceptance without condition. There is joy in accepting who you are.
11. Speak not unless it is out of Love. For you are the very essence of Love and in this you manifest your being.
12. Learn to Love and accept yourself always.

13. Love transcends all and controls none.
14. You are the embodiment of Love and Truth. Manifest who you are.
15. When you Love, all of life receives the Love.
16. You need to worship not the ego, but that part of you which is Love.
17. You have the strength and courage to walk away from an environment that does not serve your Spirit with the faith or knowing that there is always a path of Love and Truth before you that will lead to bliss.
18. Life is about the experience of choosing. Choose wisely.
19. Choice is your free will. To choose is to manifest the Spirit.
20. No one can take away your free will unless you choose to give it away.
21. When you are faced with a choice, it is a moment in time that may never return.
22. See the opportunity in each challenge. Let each moment be an opportunity to shine with the Light of your Spirit.
23. The only one who can wrong you is yourself.
24. You are the sum of all your experiences through your journey in time.
25. When you manifest Truth, all of life receives the blessing.
26. Let the foundation of your being be Truth.
27. Your eyes become clear when you accept the challenge of Truth.
28. The answer you need will come to you when you are ready.
29. When you need answers, seek within. It is the true source of your guidance. There is no other who knows you better.
30. Go into the world with spiritual purposefulness.
31. Be not controlled by the words, thoughts and deeds of others.
32. What others think of you is not as important as what you think of yourself. Value your values. Choose wisely in each moment for what you hold within goes with you into eternity. These are the eternal treasures.
33. Use the mind instead of the mind using you.

34. The heart will guide you and the mind will manifest this guidance as you command it to do so.
35. Learn to recognize mind and Spirit, know the difference and honour both.
36. Speak up, but from the heart, the source of your loving Truth.
37. Accept not the judgment of others, which creates boundaries and limits the expression of your Spirit.
38. Maintain your power for you are the sole commander of your being.
39. In difficult situations, your Spirit is being challenged. Realize that you have validity. Realize that you have power. With this power, resonate with your validity and it will lead you to a state of bliss.
40. Depend on yourself, for you are the only one you can truly depend on.
41. The one you can change is yourself; do so, for you cannot change another, unless by example.
42. Ignore the fear of the unknown for the fullness of life exists when you embrace this region.
43. Let not your fear dictate who you are.
44. You are worthy of all that you desire. Realize that it is Spirit that defines your desires.
45. To affect change, you need to take the action.
46. Have the courage to shine the Light of your Spirit in all your words, thoughts and deeds.
47. Choose from your heart, not being controlled by the thoughts, desires and emotions of others.
48. When you speak, use the simple, gentle, quiet and pure Truth.
49. Take time each day to meditate and feel the Light of life within.
50. As you meditate, in the silence of your stillness embrace that part of you, which is your God within.
51. Find that state of perfect calm, of silence, where you are in command and in touch with God.
52. If it is the desire of your Spirit and it will not hurt anyone, then just do it.

Commentary

Have you seen the Truth? Do you feel the words of Truth flow within your veins as they become part of you? Have you gained what this book has offered? If you feel that you have not, then yes, read it again, then re-read it once more. You will find treasures. Where are these treasures? They are in your heart.

You are the treasure which you seek. It is within. If you have not realized this, then read this book again, then re-read it once more. Look upon it as a series of Truths, presented as lessons, reflections, meditations and prayers, which will help you open the door to the treasures which you hold within.

Life is truly amazing. You are amazing. You are like a sparkling diamond seeking to shine and not remain hidden under a bushel. The secret of life is about removing this basket so you may shine and feel the Light that you are. You are worth it. You are worthy of it. Take the time and patience to live the life that you were born to live and feel joy. This book offers nothing unless you are willing to commit your whole life to finding the real you, your essence.

When you realize that you no longer need this book or any book and all the treasures of life lie within, then you have become an enlightened being. Embrace all that you are, and it is bliss. There is so much to tell, but they will be only empty words until you yourself feel them within your own heart.

It is my hope that you have felt Love pouring out from within these pages. Love is everywhere and you are a crucible of Love.

Love makes your diamond shine. Therefore, beloved friends, shine blissfully with every breath. It is who you are. Discover who you are. Discover all that you are and live. It is life. It is your life. To drink from the fountain of life is simply a choice. Choose life. Choose Love. Choose all that you are. Embrace the pure essence of all. Then go forth with joy on your journey, with the blessing of all that exists. Amen.

Source of Information

Search no more for there is no bibliography. The material in this book simply evolved from my life experiences. The many teachers I encountered on my journey along the way who offered Truth that touched my Spirit and guided my path have blessed me. I have learned that if you seek earnestly, patiently and diligently, you will find all that you truly need. Life is everywhere; you need only to close your eyes to see it, feel it, realize it and embrace it. It is a journey of growth. Where do you find your teacher? Embark earnestly on this journey and they will come. Like teachers, lessons also come in so many mysterious ways. Then one day perhaps you will also look at your life experiences as a book of Truth.

1. In my early years, much of my life was based on the works of Edgar Cayce, who founded the Association for Research and Enlightenment, with headquarters in Virginia Beach, USA.
2. My experiences with friends and loved ones created challenges, which offered many difficult Truths.
3. Children are a source of amazing, innocent truth.
4. Programs of study with many loving teachers helped me awaken from sleep.
5. Particularly noteworthy was a powerful aboriginal teacher and shaman. Together with her friends, she offered much to give me hope in the essence of life.
6. There is much Truth hidden between the covers of the Bible. The references in this book are based on the King James Version.

"The student becomes the teacher.
It is the way of cycles."

www.ingramcontent.com/pod-product-compliance
Lightning Source LLC
Chambersburg PA
CBHW061041110426
42740CB00050B/2527